0065691

D0560641

WITHDRAWN

DATE DUE

MAY 2 0 1993	
APR — 4 1994	
APR 25 1994	

Put It
in a Memo

Put It in a Memo

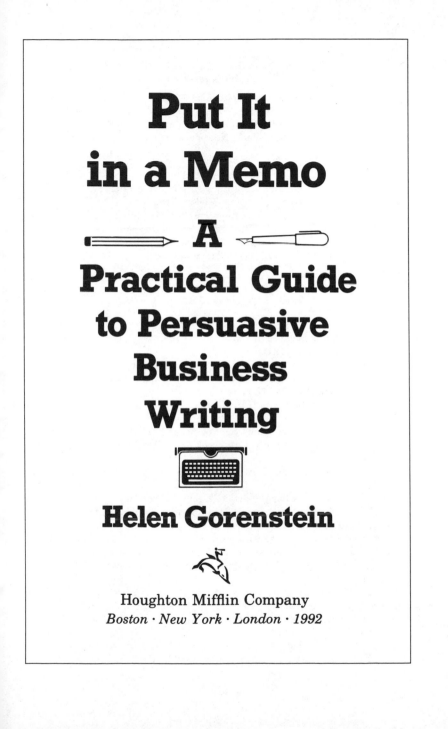

A
Practical Guide
to Persuasive
Business
Writing

Helen Gorenstein

Houghton Mifflin Company

Boston · New York · London · 1992

For information about permission to reproduce
selections from this book, write to Permissions,
Houghton Mifflin Company, 215 Park Avenue South,
New York, New York 10003.

Library of Congress Cataloging-in-Publication Data

Gorenstein, Helen.
Put it in a memo : a practical guide to persuasive
business writing / Helen Gorenstein.
p.   cm.
Includes index.
ISBN 0-395-57648-2
1. Business writing.   2. Memorandums.   I. Title.
HF5718.3.G67   1992   91-27197
651.7'55 — dc20   CIP

Printed in the United States of America

BP 10 9 8 7 6 5 4 3 2 1

Acknowledgment is made to the following for their kind permission to reprint
previously published material:

Consumers Union, for part of an article on cottage cheese published in the
Consumer Reports, July 1979. Copyright © 1979 by Consumers Union of United
States, Inc., Mount Vernon, N.Y. 10553.

Fortune, for the article *The U.S.: Team at the Top of No. 2,* by Alex Taylor
III, *Fortune,* November 9, 1987, © 1987 by Time Inc. All rights reserved.

Newsweek, for the article "Household Worries," by Peter Gwynne, *Newsweek,*
October 31, 1977, and © 1977 by Newsweek, Inc. All rights reserved. Reprinted
by permission.

The New Yorker, for the drawing by Ziegler, © 1978 by The New Yorker
Magazine, Inc.

The New York Times, for the article "Moby Balloon," by David Royce, *New
York Times Magazine,* May 26, 1974. Copyright © 1974 by The New York
Times Company. Reprinted by permission.

Bantam Books, for the excerpt from *Iacocca: An Autobiography,* by Lee
Iacocca and William Novak. Copyright © 1984 by Lee Iacocca. Reprinted by
permission of Bantam Books, a division of Bantam Doubleday Dell Publishing
Group Inc.

William Morrow & Co., for the excerpt from *Leadership and the One Minute
Manager,* by Kenneth Blanchard, Patricia Zigarmi, Drea Zigarmi. Copyright
© 1985 by Blanchard Management Corp. Reprinted by permission of William
Morrow & Co., Inc.

HarperCollins Publishers, for the excerpt from *Managing in Turbulent
Times,* by Peter F. Drucker. Copyright © 1980 by Peter F. Drucker.

Acknowledgments

Many people helped shape my concepts and approach to administrative writing. I appreciate the opportunity that I had to teach the writing workshops at Princeton University for nearly twenty years and the freedom to develop the material with intelligent comments from the staff members who participated. In particular, I want to thank Stanley Adelson, director of training and development, for his strong interest in and support of the program.

Of the many friends who discussed the material for the book in its formative stages, I especially wish to thank Gloria Levitas, Peggy Charren, Barbara Solow, and Jennifer Smith Hayden, who read sections of the book in early runs, made wise suggestions, and gave me warm support.

I am also grateful to my editor, Erika Mansourian, for her thoughtful reading of the manuscript and her patient guidance. As someone who has often been on the other side, I recognize her imaginative editing, the combination of a critical eye and a sympathetic ear that made it a pleasure to have her as my editor. For her optimistic outlook as I embarked on this project and her steadfast support during the writing, I thank my agent, Bonita K. Nelson.

Finally, I want to thank my family, not just for their encouragement during the writing of this book, but for their faith in me during my whole career. I am perhaps especially blessed to have a husband who is a mathematician and whose logical left brain served as a valuable balance to my right brain thinking. To Diana, Mark, Phyllis, and Julia I owe special thanks for their individual ways of showing love and for helping me to grow along with them.

— *Helen Gorenstein*

Contents

Introduction

Put It in a Memo is for anyone who writes on the job. These days that includes just about everyone: supervisors, administrators, managers, executives, accountants, engineers, technicians, and secretaries. The ability to write successful memos has become a measure of professional skill.

Taking an innovative approach to business communications, *Put It in a Memo* shows you how to develop your ideas on paper in the same way you would in conversation. The book introduces a step-by-step process that lets you write your thoughts clearly, concisely, and with personal warmth. These three qualities are considered the most important aspects of a good memo. You'll learn how to brainstorm your ideas on paper, capture your readers' attention, organize your information, and develop a personal style.

These strategies will help you weed out wordiness and pompous language and let you select the right words to say exactly what you mean. You'll determine what the purpose of your memo really is and learn to organize your ideas into logical patterns that your readers can follow easily. You'll recognize that the same multistage process goes on when you brainstorm your ideas at meetings or explain yourself in a discussion. When you begin to talk about an idea, you don't have all your thoughts neatly formulated. The same is true when you write a memo.

The book starts with a warm-up exercise that encourages you to suspend your critical judgment. Your goal when you begin to write is to set down quickly as many ideas as you can through random associations. Later you'll learn to evaluate your ideas, to organize them into structured patterns, and to correct grammatical errors. After all, if you're too concerned about proper punctuation and impressing your boss and colleagues when you begin to write, you can't think about what you really want to say. Your creative thinking gets stifled.

Many people have the impression that creativity applies only to poets, composers, and artists. But you're creative each time you express yourself in a fresh way. In corporations and government agencies, that creativity shows up in the innovative ways you put your thoughts on paper.

In the past two decades, information technology has exploded into the business world. As a result, the ability to write creatively, to explore and develop ideas on paper, has become a critical skill. In the old carbon-copy office, not many people saw your memos. Duplicates bleeding blue ink were cranked out by hand on a mimeograph machine, and producing more than five copies was a cumbersome chore.

Today, in the vast majority of offices, people communicate in electronically written messages that blur the distinction between original and copy. Information is swapped with no more privacy than talking on a party line in the country. Microterminals, PCs, word processors, electronic mail, fax machines — each advance in technology allows you to transmit information instantaneously and simultaneously to large groups of people. No wonder inexperienced managers and even seasoned executives are sometimes uneasy about the image they create in their memos.

Put It in a Memo is aimed at intelligent people who can make decisions but need the skills to write clearly and forcefully. Valuable ideas remain locked up inside them because they cannot express themselves on paper. A supervisor staring at blank employee evaluation forms on her desk may mutter, "How do I put my thoughts into words?" A salesperson armed with a new microterminal connected to the central computer at headquarters may ask, "How am I supposed to organize my notes about calls on my key accounts and competitors' activities?" A production manager may bury the technique for a new process in a long memo that no one can wade through.

For many people, the most daunting part of corporate life is the paperwork connected with their job. They write in a formal and impersonal style filled with "businessese" and little individuality. Some are able to get down only a few brief sentences, the barest outline with neither details nor description, so they cannot report a situation accurately or make a convincing case. When they are faced with the blank page or empty screen, ideas they expressed earlier with few hemmings and hawings fade. Others attack their material by starting anyplace, beginning in the middle of their thoughts and putting down ideas in random order. This is fine if the information is then organized and edited. But if it is left in its initial form, the readers will be as lost in the jungle of ideas as the writer was.

A request made over the telephone, a complaint aired in a coworker's office, a recommendation stated over lunch, or a proposal outlined in a committee meeting must eventually be put down on paper. Moreover, an initial discussion may have only laid the foundation. What follows is the difficult task of convincing readers of the validity of your ideas. It is essential that you express yourself clearly and persuasively.

In one sense, everyone can write. It requires only sitting down at a desk with paper and pencil or at a computer. Indeed, some people do write easily. But many find that their words do not flow effortlessly. Can someone be taught to write effectively? Yes, certainly. The people who took my writing courses learned, and so can you.

Put It in a Memo uses the scientific advances about the way the brain processes information to explore the critical stages of communicating on paper. An integral part of the book is its step-by-step writing process, based on studies in the biological and behavioral sciences about the brain's right and left hemispheres. In the late 1960s, scientists realized that the brain does not process information in a direct and orderly fashion, and their studies altered our attitudes about creativity and logical thinking. Experiments revealed that the two sides of the brain performed different tasks: one was the center of intuition and the other of logical thinking. In language, the creative right side spontaneously associates random words, draws pictures in our mind, and hears intonations, while the analytical left side selects and organizes thoughts and understands grammar and syntax.

Of course, scientists know that while the right side generates imagination, rhythm, and imagery, and the left side organization and sequential relations, there is constant communication between both hemispheres. No complex function can be assigned to one side or the other. Most people were taught to write before these discoveries were made. And many still write their memos the old-fashioned way. They worry about grammar and punctuation before they translate their ideas into words. And they assume that because they are writing about a topic they know well, their thoughts are going to take a neat, linear progression. But by challenging an overdependence on logical reasoning and the fear of making mistakes in proper English usage, you can be free to think creatively.

The techniques used in *Put It in a Memo* have been developed in writing workshops offered in government, businesses, and academia since 1975. The writing process has been tested on almost two thousand managers, executives, computer specialists, engineers, and other professionals who took the training programs during this period. All the sample memos were adapted from actual ones written in real organizations. Taken from typical situations in the workplace together with self-help worksheets, they illustrate common problems and stumbling blocks faced by business writers. They were chosen to present specific techniques and strategies to make writing memos easier. You'll learn advanced methods for stimulating your ideas, structuring your thoughts, and achieving clear, crisp copy.

Put It in a Memo is designed to help people use their creativity and organizational ability to acquire the skills they need to communicate persuasively in the practical world. One of those persuaders could be you.

Put It
in a Memo

(1)

Getting Started

- Warm up with an exercise
- Talk to your readers
- Capture all your thoughts
- Be imperfect
- Play with your ideas

When a bright young man named Michael Perkins was promoted to a management position in a large organization, he telephoned his family and friends to tell them the good news. Picking up the telephone and talking was second nature to Michael. He was comfortable expressing his ideas to clients and associates on the phone. At the food processing corporation where he worked, he made small talk and conducted important discussions with equal effectiveness — and he always listened carefully.

But in the next few weeks Michael discovered that his new job required effective writing skills. He had to be able to communicate his ideas on paper.

Sitting at his desk, he recalled requests he had made forcefully on the phone, recommendations he had outlined in a colleague's office, good suggestions he had raised at a meeting.

"Put it in a memo," the people in his company said.

Now the words escaped him. Where should he begin?

Ideas he expressed confidently in conversations and meetings were tangled in his head when he tried to write them down. The last time he had done any serious writing was in college. Now, however, he had to explain his suggestion to his supervisor about changing the distribution system. Then, too, several people in the company had to be persuaded of the new project's merit.

In conversations he often relied on nonverbal signs. He recognized that a raised eyebrow might indicate skepticism, an "uh-huh" show disbelief, or a glance out the window signal boredom. But when writing his memos, he had no such direct feedback. It was difficult to express his thoughts properly. After a few sentences, the critic in his head berated him, "That doesn't sound good to me. I don't think you started off well."

He remembered his teachers in school telling him that writing should sound impressive. He wondered how his boss, Carter Craig, was reacting to his memos. He worried about what everyone in the organization would think when they read his communications. He was stymied. Should his memos be long or short? And how detailed should they be?

Michael began to dread the task of writing and put it off as long as possible.

Sometimes Michael came across memos he thought

were effective. He read them carefully, hoping to uncover their secret. Good memos seemed like cakes with many ingredients that gave them various flavors. Some were witty and others serious, some were casual and others formal, some were long and others brief. He searched for a common quality among them, but it eluded him.

Michael began to think he would never find a way to write easily. So he chewed on the end of his pencil, watered the plant on his windowsill, or poured himself another cup of coffee. Sometimes, when he felt particularly discouraged, he wandered through the long, carpeted corridors of his sprawling building.

One afternoon he strayed farther than usual and found himself in a section where he had never been. On either side of the hallway were a number of small cubicles. At the doorway of cubicle 313, he saw a cartoon taped above a desk.

As Michael laughed, a voice behind him said, "That's to help me when I begin to write. The cartoon reminds me to let my imagination play around when I'm writing my first draft. I don't try to be logical when I start a memo, because that inhibits my creative thinking."

• Learn to listen to the right hemisphere of your brain to generate new ways of expressing your ideas. Some people think memos need to be dull and dry, but that's not true. Creative thinking lets you explore your random thoughts. Every time you discover a different approach or express yourself with a fresh perspective, you're being creative!

• 4 •

I settled into the plush violet seat, ~~by~~ my back to the great window overlooking Cold Spring Harbor. The famous man offered me a cup of tea, which I gratefully accepted. His vast mustaches drooped nearly to his ~~breast~~ ~~chest~~ ~~stomach~~ lapels, his unruly ^white hair ~~dancing~~ ~~prancing~~ shimmering in the noonday sun. (?) His noble presence seemed to fill the room ~~like a~~ ~~much as a~~ ~~not unlike a~~. My soul ~~wafted aloft~~ soared as he spoke. "So you want to be a writer," he said. "Yes," I stammered, "I ~~believe~~ fancy I do."
ZIEGLER

"I haven't got what it takes to be a writer," Michael said. "Too much paperwork comes with the title."

"What do you think it takes?" Kate Vincent asked. She had met many people who found it painful to put their thoughts on paper.

"A writer is someone who's born with a way with words."

"What makes you believe that myth?" she asked. "Do you think there's one proper set of words for writing and another for conversation?"

"In school we got better grades if we used big words," Michael said. "And if we make mistakes when we talk, they aren't on paper to embarrass us later."

- In the real world, people write to communicate their ideas. That's different from writing to sound important. To *inquire* or *request* may seem more impressive than to *ask*, but it is less straightforward, too.

"Correctness is important," Kate agreed. "But when you start to write, try not to be too critical of yourself."

"Beginnings are the hardest," Michael admitted. "I wait for inspiration."

Kate gave a quick laugh. "That's another myth about writing. And it's a dangerous concept, too, because it gives you the helpless feeling that there isn't anything you can do. Writing doesn't come from outside ourselves. It's an interior process. That isn't to say that some people don't have more writing ability than others. But good business writers follow a few basic principles. They keep their writing simple. They don't use stuffy language or trite expressions. They immerse themselves in their topic and write the way they speak."

Michael began to relax. He thought himself lucky to have found someone who knew so much about writing.

Warm Up with an Exercise

"My thoughts get tangled as soon as I try putting them on paper," he said, explaining his dilemma. "After a few sentences, I think I should have begun somewhere else."

"Isn't that the way our thinking becomes clear?" Kate asked. "Some people are like whiz kids who perform complicated mathematics in their heads. They do their brainstorming while they're shaving or putting on makeup. Or driving in their cars. But I prefer to put my thoughts on paper so there's some ground under me. Then I'm not just winging it."

- When we talk, our ideas are not neatly organized. Often we begin someplace, realize we've missed a point, backtrack, and explain ourselves more fully. When you write a memo, warm up with an exercise. Take ten minutes to write quickly on your subject. Don't stop to edit or correct. Let your ideas come out helter-skelter, without any order or organization, as though you were actually talking, trying to convince someone on the telephone or in a meeting.

Talk to Your Readers

"I'm good at explaining my ideas verbally. As a matter of fact, my best ideas occur in face-to-face discussions,"

Michael said. "When I'm writing, I miss that give-and-take."

"Writers need to pretend they're talking to their readers. But often they carry on a monologue. They write only about what interests them, putting down everything that led them to write their memos, without giving any thought to the people who will be getting them. And many people write in a way that would never be tolerated in conversation. They resort to hyper-legal-ese, jargon, and gobbledygook because they don't have confidence in their natural speaking voice."

Kate searched on her desk for a memo she had received that day and handed it to Michael. He read:

TO: All supervisors
FROM: F. P. Johnson
DATE: October 16, 1991
SUBJECT: Toxic Materials

Our office is required to annually update the names of those people, who according to the latest information available in our office, are using or regularly working in the vicinity of "toxic materials." Our listing is based on information previously provided and on supplemental information which may have been acquired. Every reasonable effort has been made in our office to keep the listing current, but a periodic and explicit updating is needed to insure its accuracy.

In the interest of the continuity of our program, you are asked to review, correct, annotate, sign and return the list to our office at your earliest convenience. Provide the names of new employees, and their starting dates, who are using or regularly working in the vicinity of sources of "toxic materials," but who do not appear on the present list. Make certain the type of work is specified and the machines used by female workers. Delete from the list those persons no longer using toxic materials and/or those who have severed their relationship with your department, indicating the cessation or termination date as appropriate. Be certain to include your name as a user on the list if appropriate.

Your help and cooperation is appreciated.

"Many people plowing through these paragraphs are going to ask themselves, 'What does Johnson want from me?' "

"How would you write it?" Michael asked.

Kate said she would use words that were part of her own everyday vocabulary, as though she were talking to her readers. And she proceeded to do so.

TO: All supervisors
FROM: F. P. Johnson
DATE: October 16, 1991
SUBJECT: Toxic Materials

You can help us update our information on people working with or near sources of toxic materials. For your convenience, a copy of your most recent list of toxic materials workers is attached. Below is an explanation of what we would like you to do and why.

1. Review the list and add or delete names as appropriate.
2. Provide starting and termination dates, which help us define a worker's period of exposure.
3. Indicate the employee's sex so that we can meet special federal and state regulations that apply to female workers.

4. If you personally work with toxic materials, be sure your name is on the list.
5. Please sign and date the form. Thanks.

"People sometimes wonder why they don't receive replies to their requests for information. But which memo would get your attention if you found it in your in-box?"

Michael grinned. "Do you have other tips on writing memos?"

Capture All Your Thoughts

"When I begin to write, I don't censor myself. I write down every idea that comes into my mind just as quickly as I can. I grab at expressions and let my words pour out."

"Doesn't it matter where I begin?" Michael persisted.

"Start anyplace — in the middle or at the end. You're creating now, not editing. Your aim at this point is simply to get all your thoughts on paper. When we talk, we stray from our subject when one thought suggests another. Often digressions contain valuable ideas. If something comes to mind, I've found I'm better off putting it down on paper."

"You mean you actually *think* on paper?"

Kate nodded. "I didn't always write that way. But I found I became too attached to particular expressions. Sometimes they led me in the wrong direction. I would write a whole memo and discover I hadn't said what I meant."

  • When you begin, use sentence fragments, run-on sentences, improper constructions — anything that lets you capture your thoughts. Writing down your ideas in imperfect English isn't murdering the language. It's a technique that lets your meaning emerge *during* the writing process.

Be Imperfect

"But what about mistakes in grammar and all the other rules?" Michael asked.

"You'll have time to worry about your diction and the fine points of language later. Let yourself be imperfect. Many people waste their time striving for words that are commonly called business-ese. They write *prior to* instead of *before* or *concerning* rather than *about*. This sort of writing is actually frowned on in today's business world. People are expected to express themselves in ways that reflect their own personality. After all, isn't that how we dress? We're not all wearing gray flannel suits."

• Anxiety can keep you from writing. Your critical side, the left hemisphere of your brain, is trained to analyze and reason; it expects perfection and interferes with your creative thinking. The hardest part is learning to turn off the critic. Recognize that clumsy phrases and awkward expressions are part of your original thought process. They're the building blocks of your initial thinking.

Play with Your Ideas

"Get it down. Then get it right! Let your imagination play around in your first draft. It's easier to write and then revise than stare at a blank sheet of paper or an empty screen," Kate said. "Just remember, getting your ideas down is the first strategy for easing the pain of writing memos."

Returning to his office, Michael listed Kate's five principles in a notebook to serve as useful reminders. He felt comforted knowing that the next time he sat down to write, he would have a new method for getting started.

(2)

Focusing on Your Readers

- Let your thoughts incubate
- Become your readers
- Tell why you're writing
- Recognize your key ideas
- Be specific
- Define your code words

Michael fired off several memos. Using his new method, he set down his thoughts exactly as they occurred to him. But something was not right. Michael was summoned to the office of his supervisor, Carter Craig.

Tapping a finger on one of Michael's memos, Carter asked, "What is this about?"

Michael read:

TO: Carter Craig
FROM: Michael Perkins
DATE: October 21, 1991
SUBJECT: Assistant Position

We have two administrative positions in Department B, one in the front office and the other in the shipping room. The person who had the position in the office has left to work elsewhere. We have another worker who is a dependable person with a pleasant personality. I would like to recommend him for the position of assistant to the sales manager. His name is Fred Harrison. Harrison has worked in the department since March, and we are pleased with the job he is doing.

"It's a recommendation," Michael explained. "I'm suggesting Fred Harrison for the opening of assistant to the sales manager."

"Well, why didn't you tell me that at the beginning of the memo?" Carter exclaimed. "I can't waste my time reading about the person who had the job before, now can I?"

What would Kate have to say about this? Michael wondered, as he found his way to her office. Taking the crumpled memo from his pocket, he asked, "Can you figure out what went wrong here?"

"Getting your ideas down is the first step," she observed. "But if you want to reach your readers, you need to put yourself in their place. Focusing on your readers is the second step in writing a good memo."

Let Your Thoughts Incubate

"Brainstorming your ideas without worrying about their order lets you explore what you want to say," Kate explained. "When you finish a first draft, set it aside. If it's an important memo, you might try leaving it for several hours while you attend to other matters. When you look at it again, you'll have a fresh perspective."

• The mind often resolves issues when you're not thinking about them. Putting a first draft aside for a short time lets you hook into the right hemisphere of your brain — your intuitive thinking. Professional writers think of the process as letting their ideas rest and incubate.

Become Your Readers

Kate offered Michael the following advice:

Good writing is a two-way process, an exchange between writer and reader. But many people write only about their own concerns instead of anticipating and responding to questions their readers would ask in a conversation. They set down everything that led them to write their memo.

When you talk with someone, you expect to be interrupted with questions if your points are not clear. Or, if you are verbose or digress, your listeners tell you to stick to the point. With written communications you have no such direct feedback. You don't have a second chance to alter a presentation or clarify an issue. So you need to train yourself to be both the writer and reader.

• Writers must play both roles, but many people find it difficult to pretend they are their readers. So write the first draft of a memo for *yourself*. Then count the times you used *we* and *our* or *I* and *my* and turn these pronouns into *you* and *your*. Changing your focus from first to second person makes your memos reader-based.

Tell Why You're Writing

Kate picked up Michael's recommendation and said, "When you are part of an organization, target your information for your readers. Find the most important sentence in your memo."

Michael reread his memo. " 'I am pleased to recommend Fred Harrison for the position of assistant to the sales manager.' "

"Put that sentence first. Don't bury it in the middle of your memo," Kate advised.

Michael shifted uncomfortably in his chair. "But in a memo like mine, isn't it boring to begin 'I am pleased to recommend Fred Harrison for the position of assistant to the manager'?"

"Not at all," Kate said. "There's a well-known adage that says, Write to express your ideas, not to impress your readers. Besides, as you become more at ease in your writing, you'll discover other ways of expressing yourself. For example, you might begin, 'Since the position of assistant to the sales manager is an important one, I have given it careful consideration. My first choice is Fred Harrison for several reasons.' Or, less formally, 'I've batted around names of candidates for assistant to the sales manager. I think that Fred Harrison is the best person for the job.' "

"Yes, I see your point," Michael said.

"Both these openings let your readers know why you

wrote the memo and also keep *you* from going off on a tangent. That's called a purpose statement. It helps you get off to a good start."

Busy people want to know right away if a memo is important to them — it's just like reading headlines in a newspaper. Headlines tell us whether we want to read the story. That's true of a memo, too.

A mystery writer can lead us along with false scents and down blind alleys, but it can be deadly for administrative writing. If your readers do not know why you're writing to them or think that what you have to say is unimportant, they may set aside your memo, intending to read it later. That sort of thing can be very costly for a company. When that happens, you end up not making the profitable impact that you might have.

The second step in writing a memo is determining your objective and letting your reader know it. Let's analyze why many people say they can express their ideas in conversation better than in writing. Isn't it because writing requires order and organization? More precision is needed in writing. But the techniques of conversation can be adapted to written communication.

As you revise your memo, let your words echo in your head and ask yourself:

Why am I sending this memo?
What do my readers need to know?
How can I get my points across?

• Here's a helpful tip for writing good beginnings. Play a mental game. Assume you have compiled in rough form all your ideas, information, and conclusions on a particular topic. Now imagine you meet your intended reader just as both of you are rushing off in different directions. You have only a minute to explain the main issue. What's the first thing you tell your reader?

Recognize Your Key Ideas

"Once you know why you're writing, it's easier to focus the attention of your readers. Remember, there's a difference between reading a memo and understanding it," Kate said. "Look at your memo and pick out your key ideas."

"What are key ideas?" Michael asked, confused.

"Key ideas are the major points that support your reason for writing. They form the scaffolding of your memo." She asked, "Why are you recommending Fred Harrison for the position of assistant to the manager?"

Michael studied his memo. " 'Harrison has worked in the department since March and we're pleased with the work he's doing. He's a dependable person with a pleasant personality.' " After a moment he added, "My key ideas don't seem very interesting."

"Nonsense," Kate replied. "You just need to develop them." Going to her filing cabinet, she handed a recommendation memo to Michael.

A RECOMMENDATION MEMO

TO: Kate Vincent
FROM: Ron Kramer
DATE: Sept. 27, 1991
SUBJECT: Account Executive/PR

I am recommending Arthur Sanders as an Account Executive in the Public Relations Department.

Sanders has been on the staff in the Marketing Division for three years. He is well organized and a self-starter. He designed several survey questionnaires that filled gaps in our knowledge about indirect competitors to our cereal line. In particular, he did a study on doughnut shops and fast-food restaurants, e.g., McDonald's.

Although Sanders is younger than most people in the department, he is mature for his age. Partly this is a matter of temperament and partly the result of being the sole support of a widowed mother. But to show the lighter side of his personality, he is a faithful member of our bowling team.

I recommend Sanders highly. I believe his innovative ideas will be an asset to the Public Relations Department.

Be Specific

"That's a well-written recommendation memo," Michael admitted.

"Yes, it follows a good format. The opening paragraph answers the question 'Why am I sending this memo?' The second paragraph discusses the person's experience, while the third one describes his personal qualities. But the key ideas are the same as yours."

Michael studied his own memo. He *had* written about Harrison's working in the department since March and also about his being dependable. "But how did Kramer develop his key ideas so well?"

"He didn't assume his readers were as familiar with his subject as he was. He asked himself, 'How can I get my points across?' " Kate said. She reminded Michael that this was the third question in taking a conversational approach to writing.

• In conversation, people are apt to choose words that their listeners can picture. But many people fail to get their points across in writing because they do not make them explicit enough. On paper, they have no confidence in their speaking voice and fill their writing with abstract words and phrases.

"If you expect your readers to understand and accept the points you're making in a memo, you need to pin down your abstractions," Kate said.

"People's experiences color the way they look at things. For one person, *office* may mean a large room with posters on the walls and windows that overlook a park, while for another it can be a small, dark space." She added, "You can't persuade your readers to your point of view if your key ideas aren't described in ways that they can picture."

"In other words, I should be specific," Michael said.

"That's right," Kate said enthusiastically. "Look at good writing. You'll see its impact comes from its concrete images and specific examples."

Define Your Code Words

- Code words: Technical terms, business jargon, acronyms, or abstract phrases that mean more to the writer than they do to the reader. They call up a host of images for the writer that the reader does not share.

"Many writers explain the key ideas in their memos with code words. For example, an engineer writing about an environmental audit might use the expression 'a site walkthrough.' To the engineer, the term indicates a complex network of tasks, but for the executives in a company or its legal department, who read the memo, the phrase may not bring forth any image at all," Kate said.

"I could say we work for a friendly company. Would you agree?" she asked Michael.

"Of course."

"But what do you mean by friendly?"

"There isn't a lot of formality."

Kate shook her head. "Formality is another of those abstract code words."

"Everyone in the company is on a first-name basis," Michael said after a moment's thought.

"For me, we're a friendly company because there isn't an executive dining room. Everybody eats together in the cafeteria, including our new president."

Michael saw her point. "Code words can mean something different to different people."

"That's right. A responsible worker, an interesting job,

or a mature individual are shorthand references. They're a writer's personal code and need to be defined."

Kate looked inquiringly at Michael. "How would you describe Harrison's dependability to someone who doesn't know him?"

"Harrison always has the figures for the weekly reports, which are due by five o'clock on Tuesday, on my desk before noontime of that day. He double-checks the numbers —"

Kate interrupted. "Put that information in your memo. As you brainstorm a memo, practice drawing pictures for your readers. And when you revise your draft, watch for code words."

- When you reread a memo, examine your abstract nouns or special terms to see whether they carry more meaning for you than for your average reader. Then use your code words as jumping-off points to amplify and explain your ideas.

Michael reread his recommendation memo:

TO: Carter Craig
FROM: Michael Perkins
DATE: October 21, 1991
SUBJECT: Assistant Position

We have two administrative positions in Department B, one in the front office and the other in the shipping room. The person who had the position in the office has left to work elsewhere. We have another worker who is a dependable person with a pleasant personality. I would like to recommend him for the position of assistant to the sales manager. His name is Fred Harrison. Harrison has worked in the department since March and we are pleased with the job he is doing.

Then, using Kate's hints, he revised the memo to read:

TO: Carter Craig
FROM: Michael Perkins
DATE: October 21, 1991
SUBJECT: Assistant Position

I have thought about the opening of assistant to the sales manager and my suggestion for the position is Fred Harrison.

Harrison has worked in the department since March and we are pleased with the job he is doing. He has responsibility for inventory control. He set up the current system himself, and, as you know, an up-to-date and accurate inventory count can make the difference between getting orders out on time and having dissatisfied customers.

He is a dependable person with a pleasant personality. He always has the figures for the weekly reports, which are due on Tuesday afternoon, on my desk by noontime. On the few occasions when it has been necessary to work overtime, he always pitches in willingly.

I believe Harrison is ready for a promotion and I recommend him highly for the position of assistant to the sales manager.

Michael was surprised at how well his memo turned out and thanked Kate for her help.

"You did it yourself. Focusing on your readers is the second step in writing a memo," she reminded him.

(3)

Planning Your Memo

- Preview your points
- Group similar ideas
- Set up a writing route
- Map your mind
- Develop shared goals

Michael was writing with greater ease. On his computer, he imagined he was talking to his readers and immersed himself in his topic. He highlighted his key ideas.

At a weekly department meeting, Carter Craig announced that the company was changing to a new telephone system. Michael returned to his office and wrote the following memo:

TO: Carter Craig
FROM: Michael Perkins
DATE: November 4, 1991
SUBJECT: Telephones

Since the new telephone system is going into effect soon, now is a good time to have a telephone relocated. There are two phones on the administrator's desk and none for the copy room. Frequently he spends several hours in the copy area.

One further *important* request. We have a telephone that is used exclusively with our terminal and computer. This phone has a white sticker on its base and is numbered sequentially with our other phones. Does this indicate it will be part of the new system? I hope it will not, because the very reason we have this instrument is due to the fact that the terminal cannot be used with a phone system. Would you please check into this, because it is essential that there be an operating phone for our computerized inventory searching. Also, it would be an enormous convenience for the administrator to have a phone in the copy room. Shall I assume the relocation of the phone will take place when it can be arranged?

Carter responded, approving the transfer of the phone to the copy area. He did not reply, however, to the question about the telephone used with the terminal and computer. Michael felt he had made two equally important requests but received Carter's assurance on only one of them.

Puzzled, he went to Kate Vincent's office and showed her the memo. "Carter missed my second point. He didn't mention my request about the computer phone."

"That sometimes happens with busy people," Kate said. She motioned Michael to take a seat.

Preview Your Points

"Busy people often get interrupted while they're reading a memo," Kate said.

As Michael considered this, she looked at the memo. It was too wordy. Thirteen words could be cut from a very long sentence: 'the very reason we have this instrument is due to the fact that.' When you're adding a point or stating a reason, you don't need to announce it. Inflated clauses and dreary phrases tend to bore or distract your reader.

"Look at your memo again," Kate suggested. "If you were covering two topics, why didn't you tell Carter at the outset?"

Michael reread his memo. "I suppose if the second topic was that important, I should have stated in my opening paragraph: 'I have two requests to make before the new telephone system takes effect.' "

• First paragraphs should brief your readers on *everything* you'll be saying in your memo. That way they don't end up missing key points. Good organization can turn a bad memo into a good one.

Group Similar Ideas

"Generally, writers know why they're sending a memo, but often they don't organize their thoughts for their readers," Kate said. "That involves using the logical left side of the brain. Our analytical thinking.

"The ability to write persuasively depends on the ability to think logically. Your memo reads as though you went to a supermarket with a list that hadn't been put in any order. You keep crisscrossing and retracing your steps."

Michael considered his memo and agreed. "How do you plan a writing itinerary?"

Kate laughed. "When you're generating ideas, you begin anywhere, don't you? You jot down your thoughts as they occur to you. But if you expect your readers to follow you, you need to sort your random thoughts into categories."

• The left hemisphere of the brain is always analyzing and making categories. Otherwise we wouldn't make sense of anything. Of course, there isn't one right way to classify our thoughts. We each devise our own system.

Kate explained that she generally did her brainstorming on the back of an old envelope. Then she examined her list and asked herself what were the critical issues she wanted to cover in her memo.

"For example, if someone were asked to make recommendations for modernizing our canning facility, they might gather information about our present production capabilities into one pile, ways of improving safety into a second, advances in technology into a third, and so forth."

"They group similar ideas," Michael exclaimed, catching on.

"That's right. These categories become focal points of their paragraphs."

Set Up a Writing Route

"After you've sorted your thoughts into categories, you want to make a kind of map to lead your readers in the right direction. You want to be certain that your readers arrive at the right destination. That depends on your analytical thinking, too," Kate said.

"You mean so that readers understand and respond to everything in my memo?"

Kate nodded in agreement. "You need to guide your readers through the maze of your writing. My old boss was a stickler for the well-organized memo. He was always saying, 'First, get your ideas down, then organize them.' "

• Posting road markers is one way to let your readers know the various points you'll cover in a memo. Guideposts help your readers recognize your main points and also alert them when you digress or take a fork in the road. They help organize your own thinking, too. Your key ideas are the critical points in your memo. They become your major stopping places along the way. Formats, visual cues, headings, and topic sentences are road signs that your readers watch for along the way.

FORMATS

The format of a memo helps target your message for yourself and your readers.

The To: line makes you decide before you start to write who is going to get your memo. Often memos are sent to more than one person in an organization. With today's document processing and electronic mail systems, messages can automatically be routed to everyone who needs to see them.

The FROM: line lets your readers know quickly who sent the message.

The DATE: line orders the memo chronologically.

The SUBJECT: line is generally an abbreviated version of your purpose statement and tells your reason for the communication. If you seriously intend to communicate with your readers, your SUBJECT: lines should be as specific as possible. Telephone System Changes is a more precise subject head than Telephones. It lets your reader know why you are sending the memo and focuses attention on your subject.

VISUAL CUES

Visuals are ways of designing your memo so that your eye does half the thinking for the brain. Some ways of constructing visuals are:

· Using bullet marks.
· Putting headings in capital letters.
· Underlining certain words.
· Indenting specific examples.
· Leaving extra white space.
· Adopting a different typeface.
· Setting up rows and columns.

An easily read design can emphasize the points you are making and can make the difference between getting a response to your message and having your memo end up in the pile to be looked at later.

Here's a memo with a solid text.

TO: Kate
FROM: Steve
DATE: November 6, 1991
SUBJECT: Travel Expenditures

From Tuesday, October 8, until Thursday, October 10, I attended the Midwest Food Show in Chicago. From Chicago I traveled to Detroit to attend the Food Packaging Trade Conference. (The FPTC is a regional workshop/conference — October 11–12.) I submitted an advance request for travel expenses to attend the Chicago Food Show and was reimbursed $1,300. This leaves me $491 in the red. Plane tickets were $1,054.50; other travel $30. Accommodations: 3 nights in Chicago — $243; 2 nights in Detroit — $152. Food for 5 days — $311.50. Travel bills and receipts are attached. I would like to present a claim for my additional expenses.

And here's the revised version, with its points emphasized through visual cues:

TO: Kate
FROM: Steve
DATE: November 6, 1991
SUBJECT: Additional Travel Expenses

I am requesting reimbursement for added expenses incurred when I attended the Food Packaging Trade Conference in Detroit on October 11–12, as well as the

Midwest Food Show in Chicago. My initial travel vouchers covered only the trip to the Midwest Show. Actual travel costs were:

TRANSPORTATION:
Plane tickets	$1,054.50
Buses and taxis	30.00

ACCOMMODATIONS:
Chicago (3 nights)	243.00
Detroit (2 nights)	152.00

FOOD:
Five (5) days	311.50
	$1,791.00

I received an advance of $1,300.00, which leaves a balance of $491. The enclosed vouchers and log sheets verify my expenses.

HEADINGS

Headings announce your various topics in the same way that subheads do in magazine articles. They divide the information into major concepts to show your readers the topics you are covering. They let your readers skim a memo and grasp its parts before they read the text. Also, since headings direct attention to particular points, they provide an easy way of referring to a topic at a later time.

Here's a memo in which headings helped management find the information quickly:

TO: Production Supervisors
FROM: Manny Clark
DATE: October 30, 1991
SUBJECT: Machine-related Downtime Study

Spurred by inconsistent productivity and inordinate maintenance costs, we hired a consultant to analyze machine-related downtime. I share the following results from the initial report with you.

Mechanical Malfunctions: Mechanical malfunctions accounted for 2.4% of lost production time in machine-related downtime. Package transfer malfunctions from the station to the stacker were responsible for 1.2%. Fabric input malfunctions accounted for another .9%. Other malfunctions, too numerous to list, which were simply categorized as miscellaneous, accounted for an additional .3% of each shift.

Machine Maintenance: Maintaining the machines themselves accounted for 13.4% of lost production time. Of this amount, 5.6% was consumed in wait time for the machine operator to notify maintenance. Actual repair accounted for 7.8% of machine-related downtime.

Conclusions: Machine maintenance accounts for six times as much production downtime as mechanical malfunctioning. Almost 50% of lost production time came from waiting for machine operators to notify maintenance. The results of this study and appropriate future actions will be on the agenda of the November Production Supervisors Meeting.

TOPIC SENTENCES

That old standby, the topic sentence of a paragraph, also draws attention to the points you are making in a memo. Paragraphs are designed to group sentences around a central idea and help to break the information into readable units.

The topic sentence leads into your subject and forecasts what will follow in the rest of the paragraph. Having introduced your topic, however, you should support your readers' built-in expectations by supplying specific reasons, facts, and examples.

TO: Support Staff
FROM: Jim Parker
DATE: November 1, 1991
SUBJECT: "Business" Hours

This memo is to clarify company policies regarding the 20-minute "coffee break" and lunch hour, which normally is scheduled from noon to 1:00 p.m. or 1:00 to 2:00 p.m.

A 20-minute rest period may be taken as a single break or divided between two periods, but I ask that not everyone leave at the same time. We now have five support staff, and at least two members should be available to cover the phones at all times.

Lunch hour schedules are posted each week. It is important to return on time so that you do not delay others. Naturally, there must be flexibility, and if you wish to take a different lunchtime, please arrange to switch with someone else so that we still have good telephone coverage. If you have special plans and cannot make arrangements with someone else, check with me.

And thanks for the dedication you all showed this fall during our busy time. With our added staff member, I am confident that we will be able to keep up with the workload.

Map Your Mind

"The various points in a memo sometimes carry equal weight. For instance, in a memo listing the agenda of an upcoming meeting, the topics do not have much in common with one another," Kate said.

TO: Staff Advisory Committee
FROM: Karen Brown
DATE: November 5, 1991
SUBJECT: Personnel and Policy Plans

Our next meeting is scheduled for Thursday, November 21, at 2 p.m. The planned agenda consists of progress reports and discussions (limited to 15 minutes each) on the following issues:

- Performance evaluations
- Interdepartmental communications
- Annual Christmas party

Please come with your suggestions on these topics.

● Topics that do not have much in common with one another may be listed in any order.

"On the other hand, some writing routes are more complex. If you're trying to persuade or convince your readers to take specific action, how you choose to arrange your facts can influence their perceptions.

"Let me give you an example. I have to write a memo

requesting a six-week leave of absence for my administrative assistant. Here's the way I jotted down my ideas, but it's as though I tossed them on the floor. They haven't any order," Kate said, showing Michael her list.

> Joyce's day care arrangements fell through . . .
> The sales conference is in March, but planning starts two months before . . .
> Good attendance record . . .
> Travel arrangements for participants . . .
> Wants six-week leave to make other arrangements . . .
> Mailing lists . . .
> Been admin here five years . . .
> Slack time for our department — temps . . .

"Since day care leaves aren't company policy, I have to map my thinking and present the facts in a way that convinces the director of personnel. Mindmapping helps me plan the writing route. It lets me think creatively about the best way to organize my thoughts. It's a visual way of expressing how the brain sorts out ideas."

• Mindmapping organizes ideas on paper in a free-form diagram. It's more successful than outlining in the traditional fashion because the brain does not naturally think in roman numerals or capital and small letters. Of course, there are no general rules for mindmapping — everyone arranges thoughts differently — but here are a few guidelines.

1. Draw a circle in the center of a piece of paper.
2. Write your purpose for sending the memo inside the circle.

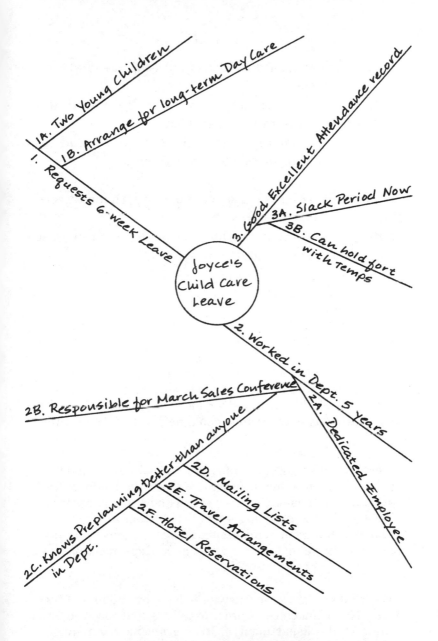

Mindmapping Plan

3. Put down your key ideas in lines that radiate from the circle.
4. Develop subpoints on smaller lines that form branches from your key ideas.
5. Number each item to make a route or road map that sets priorities for your topics.

Kate showed Michael a sheet of paper with messy scribbling.

Later, Michael read the memo that Kate wrote based on her mindmapping plan:

TO: S. P. Sandelman
FROM: Kate Vincent
DATE: October 31, 1991
SUBJECT: Child Care Leave

I am writing to endorse a request from Ms. Joyce Banks for a six-week leave without pay beginning November 11, 1991. Ms. Banks has asked for the leave to make suitable long-term day care arrangements for her two young children.

As Ms. Banks's supervisor for five years, I have found her to be industrious and dedicated. She is responsible for the annual March Sales Conference and knows the paperwork involved in the planning stage better than anyone else. In fact, it has been her conscientious attention to mailing lists and travel details that has made these meetings go so smoothly in the past.

Ms. Banks assures me she will be back by the first of the year. Her attendance record is excellent, and based on her value to the department, I favor granting her request. The next six weeks are a slack period in our department and we can manage with a temporary replacement. I am, therefore, recommending that the leave without pay be approved. I'll contact you in a few days to discuss details.

Develop Shared Goals

"Of course, you may have one goal in mind while your readers may be going in a completely different direction," Kate said. "Memos have to be arranged to solve problems or achieve ends your readers care about. You need to know their opinions and prejudices so that you can act on them."

"Isn't that going too far?" Michael asked. "Am I supposed to be practicing psychology or writing a memo?"

"Modern business writers do both," she replied. "They present their ideas so that they set up shared goals with their readers. They put themselves in their readers' shoes. Look at it this way. Your readers have half a dozen memos on their desk. What will make them want to read yours first?"

"I suppose they're more interested in memos that involve themselves or their department."

"That's human nature, isn't it," Kate remarked. "No one likes getting memos aimed at no one in particular."

• It's easier to understand information that's written in a context that's familiar and meaningful. A computer screen or blank sheet of paper can't make faces or gestures to remind you that you've overlooked critical points. If you wish to be persuasive, ask yourself what your readers need to know to understand your message.

Are your readers:

- Familiar with your technology and shop terms?
- Acquainted with your issues?
- In agreement with your ideas?
- Sympathetic to your goals?
- Neutral to your proposal?
- Feeling threatened by your project?

In today's business world, the trend is toward writing geared to your readers. So answers to questions like these affect how you write a memo. Your readers may be divided into two categories:

Experts. These are members of your own department who are familiar with your subject and understand the situation. Sometimes they are the people who told you to "put it in a memo." But even so-called experts do not know as much about your operation as you do, so your memos should answer all the questions they will ask — or even those they have in mind.

Decision-makers. Memos can go to one person, to several, to a committee, to top management, or end up in a case file. Quite often they are a selling device and must persuade or convince your readers. Writers sometimes slur over difficult questions, hoping their readers won't notice the omissions. But nothing weakens a memo more than missing information or hidden facts. Decision-makers will be wary of any conclusions if they feel the facts on which they are based are overstated or incomplete. You must justify your points carefully, logically, and in an unbiased manner.

"Good memos focus on your readers," Kate summed up. "Bill Fredricks was always stressing the significance of knowing who your audience is out there. He used to say find out all you can about what your readers want to know. Then organize your memos for them. He believed that writing memos was a great training device in logical thinking."

"Was Fredricks your old boss?" Michael asked. Since joining the company, he had been hearing about the legendary Bill Fredricks's power with the written word.

Kate nodded. "You ought to go talk to Bill."

"He won't mind?" asked Michael, visualizing the hallowed third floor, where the senior executives held court.

"Not at all. He'll admire your interest in wanting to know how to write better memos," Kate said. "Ask him about his menu for structuring information."

Later, when Michael returned to his office, he took a second look at his memo. Using the information he had learned about mapping his thoughts, he rewrote it.

TO: Carter Craig
FROM: Michael Perkins
DATE: November 4, 1991
SUBJECT: Telephone System Changes

With a new telephone system going into effect in several weeks, I would like to request that: (1) the second phone in the administrator's area be relocated, and (2) the telephone currently used specifically for inventory control not become part of the new system.

Relocation of a Telephone: There are two phones in the administrator's area and none in our copy room. Since the administrator frequently spends several hours in the copy room, it would be convenient to have a phone there. Can this transfer be incorporated with the change to the new system?

Computer Search Telephone: The phone used with our terminal and computer has a white sticker on its base and has been numbered sequentially with the other phones. Does that indicate it will become part of the new system? I hope not, because the terminal cannot be used with a phone system and it is essential that we have a phone for our computerized inventory searches.

Please let me know your thoughts on both matters. Thanks.

(4)

Choosing a Structure

- Arrange by topic
- Highlight with parallel construction
- Relate in chronological sequence
- Draw comparisons
- Argue with cause and effect

During the next several weeks, Michael was too busy to contact Bill Fredricks. His department was considering launching a new product, and meetings were held with people in production, marketing, and accounting.

At the end of the second week, Carter Craig asked Michael to write a memo presenting the background data and the pros and cons of the new product. The memo would be distributed widely throughout the company, because senior executives would be deciding on the feasibility of the proposed product. Carter said, too, that the memo would be part of an ongoing file, a useful reference that might even become a legal document if the company decided to take out a patent on the production technology.

Michael had never felt so swamped with information to organize. He telephoned Bill Fredricks's secretary to make an appointment and was amazed when she told him to come that afternoon.

Bill Fredricks held out his hand when Michael came in and asked, "Well, young man, what can I do for you?"

Michael described his discussions with Kate Vincent and explained that he wanted to know more about how to structure information. He pointed at a sheaf of notes he had brought with him and asked, "Do you have any suggestions on how to organize all this?"

Bill Fredricks smiled and said, "Why don't you tell me what you've got there?"

"There's background information about why we wanted to develop the product. Then there's the reasons that this product would satisfy customers' demand, based on diet and nutritional changes. And there's the results from sampling in trial marketing."

When the young man finished, the executive said, "Well, there's no need to reinvent the wheel, is there? People have been writing for a good many centuries."

● A structural design underlies all good writing. Writers can't express ideas randomly and expect their readers to follow the pattern of their thoughts. For example, writing about the space requirements in your department, you could mix and match from the following menu and structure your memo with:

· A *topical arrangement* based on the many tasks that your department is responsible for.

- A *parallel construction* that gives a quick overview of your department's activities.
- A *chronological sequence* that records the various changes in your department over the past three, five, or ten years that led to the need for additional space or that forecasts the future needs of your department.
- A *comparison method* that examines the advantages accrued from larger accommodations and the disadvantages of the current arrangement.
- A *cause-and-effect pattern* that details your present space shortage and your recommendations for improving the situation.

Arrange by Topic

"The topical arrangement is probably the most common way of arranging your ideas. With a topical ordering, you organize information by its subject. The first sentence in each paragraph tells your readers the point of the paragraph right at the start," Fredricks said.

Michael thought for a moment. "Excuse me, but aren't there circumstances when it might be best not to divulge my main point right off the bat?"

"When's that?" Fredricks asked.

"For example, if I'm discussing a problem or suggesting unpopular actions, wouldn't it be preferable to lead up to the subject?" Michael ventured.

After a pause, Fredricks said, "There's a greater chance you'll lose your readers completely by keeping them in the dark. There are sound and practical reasons for organizing memos with topic sentences."

> • In a topical arrangement, an opening sentence contains the central point of a paragraph and forecasts what will be coming. Details are added, points defined and further illuminated, based on the topic sentence. Generally, with a topical ordering, the contents of a memo can be gleaned from the opening sentence in each paragraph.

"Let's say you're writing about Cookerine, a food processor that has the following features: a considerably stronger motor, 46% more capacity than earlier models, new disks that slice food more attractively, and a better safety switch.

"An appropriate opening sentence might be: 'The new Cookerine has many improved features,' " Fredricks said. "Or, 'Our food processor is wearing a new look.' "

"I prefer the second one," Michael said.

"It's less precise. The point is, the machine is improved. Accuracy is an important rule of good writing."

With the first topic sentence the paragraphs would read: *The new Cookerine processor has many improved features*. It has a considerably stronger motor and 46% more capacity than earlier models. The new disks slice foods more attractively. And a better switch provides increased safety.

"Can we try another example?" Michael asked.

Taking a piece of paper from his desk, Fredricks read off the points he planned to cover in a memo about sales growth in the microwave foods area:

"Ten years ago 60-minute gourmet was a great concept. Now people want their dinners ready in 60 seconds. The 30-second hot fudge sundae is a hot item. The 2-minute linguine with clam sauce has arrived. The 4-minute cake mix comes complete with frosting."

"We're living in a gastronomical waistland," Michael said.

"It's catchy and has personal style," Fredricks said, "but it misses the point about fast cooking time. Occasionally topic sentences aren't the first sentence in a paragraph. Can you add another sentence that's more of an umbrella for the ideas?"

Michael tried again. "New microwave foods that have short preparation time are bringing fast foods to the kitchen."

Fredricks nodded and showed Michael two memos that had been organized in topical arrangements.

TO: Alec Penn, Vice-President/Human Development
FROM: Liz Savvy
DATE: November 12, 1991
SUBJECT: Promotion Opportunities

I would like to make several suggestions that relate to making staff members aware of job opportunities within the company.

Job Postings are currently listed in the four dining areas. Since some people eat lunch at their desks or outside the buildings, it might be helpful if current openings were posted on department bulletin boards as well.

Dial-a-Job tapes provide information about job openings 24 hours a day. Communicating computers are another way of letting people know at any time of the day about job opportunities in the company.

Performance Appraisals are a good time to discuss possibilities for promotion and advancement. Supervisors and managers could refer to management training courses within the company that offer the potential for professional growth.

I would sincerely appreciate the chance to review with you these new channels for encouraging staff development.

TO: Mr. W. Fredricks
FROM: R. V. Davis
DATE: November 15, 1991
SUBJECT: Plumbing Renovation

I am attaching for your approval an appropriations request in the amount of $1,700 for the replacement of two rather ancient sinks in the Testing Kitchen. The installation of new sinks will eliminate further maintenance expenses and a serious safety problem.

The drain in the sink on the north side of the kitchen is continuously clogged. Plumbers are called on a regular basis. We have been advised that the sink is old and the drainpipe too small to handle the present volume. Since the problem persists and water sometimes stands in the sink for several days, we would like to replace the sink and install a larger pipe to eliminate further maintenance expense.

The hot and cold water mixer in the sink on the south side of the kitchen is defective. At the present time, the water runs very hot despite the temperature control having been adjusted several times. This poses a serious safety hazard and should be attended to at once.

The proposed renovations can be completed within a month after approval and installation accomplished without any testing downtime.

Highlight with Parallel Construction

"You've probably used some of my menu for structuring information without being aware of it," said Fredricks, adding, "One of the oldest forms of structure involves expressing similar ideas in a similar form. For instance, you undoubtedly know the lines
A time to break down, and a time to build up;
A time to weep, and a time to laugh;
A time to mourn, and a time to dance;
A time to cast away stones, and a time to gather stones together. . . .

- Inexperienced writers often think they need to vary their expressions, probably from some mistaken idea that repeating the same words indicates a limited vocabulary. While there can be monotony from repetitions, parallel construction can also add consistency and strength to your writing.
  To be effective, all items in a parallel series should start with the same part of speech. This likeness of form makes it easier for your readers to understand the various points. The symmetry of parallel construction gives the analytical left hemisphere of the brain a pattern to hook onto.

Suppose you were asked to write a memo giving tips on making a presentation at a meeting. It might contain the following list:

- An outline to cover major points.
- Use audiovisual aids whenever possible.
- From time to time repeat your main points.
- Discussions should be kept brief.
- Skip unnecessary details.

Put into parallel construction, the list would read:

- Prepare an outline of your major issues.
- Reinforce your ideas with audiovisual aids.
- Emphasize your main points by repeating them.
- Keep your discussion brief.
- Skip unnecessary details.

As you can see, in the second example each item begins with a verb.

"Let's compare a memo that has been written in a block format with one set up with parallel construction," Fredricks said.

TO: All Production Managers
FROM: Controller
DATE: November 13, 1991
SUBJECT: Pay Rate Classification

The following information is offered to provide guidelines when filling temporary unskilled positions:

Determine on the attached classification sheet the hourly wage to be paid all temporary unskilled workers. Exceptions will be made only to positions that have prior approval from the Controller's Office. No rates in excess of the established hourly wage, as shown on the attached classification sheets, will be paid unless this approval is on file with the Controller's Office. If you wish a job rate to be reviewed to ensure consistency, contact the Controller's Office. The Controller's Office will add new job titles from time to time as they are deemed necessary.

TO: All Production Managers
FROM: Controller
DATE: November 13, 1991
SUBJECT: Pay Rate Classification

The attached classification sheet provides guidelines when you are filling temporary unskilled positions. Please note that:

- All positions are paid on an hourly basis.
- Only jobs with written approval may exceed the established hourly rate.
- A rate review may be requested to ensure consistency.
- New job titles will be added from time to time.

"The second memo is easier to read," Michael said. "Or I should say that it's easier to understand."

"Yes, using bullets lets you fire off your ideas. You know, our objectives are the following: bong, bong, bong, or the topics to be analyzed are bong, bong, bong."

"Kate Vincent calls them visual cues," Michael said.

"That's right," Fredricks said, handing Michael two memos formatted with bullets and using parallel construction.

TO: Distribution
FROM: L. P. Stone
DATE: October 14, 1991
SUBJECT: Safety Training

You have been selected to attend the Supervisor Safety
Training program. The dates, times, and locations are
listed below:

November 3   1:00–2:30 P.M.   Common Room
November 10   2:00–4:00 P.M.   Lab Conference Room

The following topics will be discussed:
 • *Job Safety Analysis*
    Purpose of job safety analysis
    Effective self-inspection
 • *Planned Safety Inspections*
    Inspection as management responsibility
    Basic causes of hazards

Please set aside the time to attend all the sessions. If you
have conflicts with your own schedule, call me so that we
can try to work it out.

Distribution:

M. Alberts   C. Conover   K. Martin
S. Bright   W. Landers   M. Parker

TO: All Production Managers
FROM: Charles Banks
DATE: November 19, 1991
SUBJECT: Reimbursements on F&BA Meeting

The following guidelines for reimbursement of expenses
incurred at the F&BA meeting have been established. The
Controller's Office will pay:

- Round-trip business-class air fare to St. Louis.
- Registration fee for the meeting.
- A $120 per diem to cover hotel, meals, ground transportation, and other miscellaneous expenses.

An accounting of all expenses must be submitted with your final travel voucher. If you have any questions, please contact me at ext. 2060.

● Items listed in a similar format are both easy to read and easy to follow. The vertical structure and white space create a memo that is visually appealing.

Relate in Chronological Sequence

"Choosing the correct structure helps develop your ideas," Fredricks said. "When you're writing about events that begin at a certain time and move either forward or backward, you're organizing information chronologically. Myths and fairy tales were written that way. Once upon a time, and so forth."

Michael was surprised by this connection with writing memos.

Putting thoughts in a time frame controls the way information is presented. It takes advantage of your readers' expectations. Readers like to have a trail that's carefully marked. When you mention *first,* they will be watching for *second.* If you write *at the start,* they will be looking for the next *time* word that carries your ideas forward. These cues make it easier for your readers to process your information.

- You're telling a story when your memo relates the background on a problem, recounts the history of a project, records the status of an ongoing situation, or describes the steps in a lab procedure. In all those instances, your thoughts can be organized with *time* words.

TIME WORDS

Giving a sequential ordering:	*first*
	second, etc.
	last
Looking backward:	*early on*
	in the beginning
	initially
	six months ago
Carrying thoughts forward:	*two weeks later*
	subsequently
	the following month
	after a few days
	finally

Fredricks said, "When I began writing memos, I looked at the way professional writers structured their thoughts. It seemed constructive to try to learn their techniques. I figured if someone was willing to pay them for their writing, then I should study how they did it. Professional writers frequently develop ideas in chronological sequence. Matter of fact, I still have a sample of the narrative technique." He took an article from the lower drawer of his desk and handed it to Michael.

"I recognized that certain words, such as *the first time, World War I, between 1918 and 1926, now,* and *these days*

If the high price of meat prompts consumers to switch to cottage cheese for more of their protein, it won't be the first time. Back in 1918, the U.S. Department of Agriculture began promoting cottage cheese to help alleviate the World War I meat shortage. The USDA's efforts had a lasting effect; per-capita consumption of cottage cheese doubled between 1918 and 1926 and increased still more during the World War II meat shortage. Nearly 500 million pounds were sold in 1944 alone.

By now, of course, cottage cheese has become an accepted meat substitute not only for those priced out of the meat market by inflation but also for America's permanent cadre of dieters in need of a low-calorie source of protein.

Americans buy about a billion pounds of cottage cheese a year these days; that represents roughly one-third of all the cheese sold in this country. Despite its

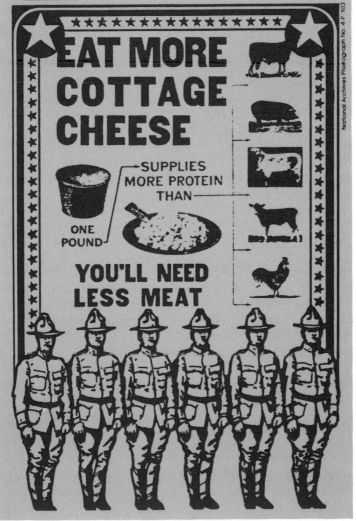

were presenting background information in a time frame. As you can see, I underlined those words.

"You can use the same technique when you're writing the part of your memo that explains what's been going on in your department during the past few years," Fredricks advised. "For instance, here's a memo that was sent to our advertising department about a new black bean soup we developed."

TO: Fred Carpenter
FROM: Nancy Lewis
DATE: October 2, 1991
SUBJECT: Marketing Release/Black Bean Soup

With the approach of winter and cold weather, now is a good time to get together to discuss our advertising campaign.

We think homemade soup still brings a smile to many people's faces, even though it has been a long time since people simmered soups on the stove. Once 19th-century technology developed the canning process, condensed soups became America's first real convenience foods. By the 1940s, cans of soup were staples in almost every pantry. Advertising at that time plugged cost and convenience rather than quality.

Today canned soup is still a convenient, low-cost staple, but now we're also looking at its nutritional value. Bean soups tested higher in protein than any other soup.

Let's get together next week to talk about testing results and market sampling. I'll call you to set up a meeting.

"Generally people aren't as familiar with the inner workings of your department as you are. They don't have the intimate knowledge of its operation that you have, so narrating the historical background provides information so they can understand and evaluate the situation."

"Do you mind if I take a copy of that memo along with me?" Michael asked. "It'll help me remember about organizing memos in a chronological sequence. I'll underline the time words for future reference."

"Good idea," Fredricks said.

Draw Comparisons

"Organizing information by drawing comparisons is another structure you probably use all the time, too, without thinking about it," Fredricks said. "For example, how about telling me about Carter Craig and your previous boss?"

Michael thought for a moment before he said, "Carter's easy to talk to. He's got a great sense of humor. He's interested in what I've got to say, and he's fair in his dealings with me, too. Not like my boss where I worked before I came here. He was very tense, although he could be funny, too. He pretended to have an open door policy, but he made all the decisions on his own."

Fredricks smiled. "Without making a conscious effort, you used comparison to structure your thoughts. First you talked about Carter's sense of humor and fairness. Then you described your former boss and showed how he was similar to and different from Carter. That same technique can be used to write an evaluation of people or products."

Fredricks showed Michael two paragraphs from an article called "Moby Balloon," which described the similarities and differences between gas and hot-air balloons.

Gas balloons swim around in air like a sleeping fish in water, because they weigh about the same as the fluid they're in. A good, big, trans-Atlantic balloon will have 2,000 pounds of vehicle, including gas bag and pilot, taking up about 30 cubic feet (as big as a refrigerator), plus 300 pounds of a "nothing" stuff called helium, which fills 30,000 cubic feet (as big as three houses). Air to fill this 30,030 cubic feet would also weigh 2,300 pounds, so the balloon system averages the same as air, floating in it as part of the wind.

Hot-air balloons use the same size bag, filled with hot air instead of helium, kept hot by a boot-sized blowtorch riding just over the pilot's head. Hot air is light, but not as light as helium, so you can't carry as much equipment in a hot-air balloon. You also can't fly as long or as far. Helium will carry a balloon for days (three and a half days is the record), until a lot of gas has leaked out. But a hot-air balloon cools down in minutes, like a house as soon as its heat source runs out of fuel; and today's best fuel (heat-for-weight), propane, lasts only several hours.

In the first paragraph, gas balloons are discussed in terms of their weight, size, and floating distance. The second paragraph, on hot-air balloons, describes these same qualities but refers to the former paragraph. Thus, *Hot air is light, but not as light as helium.* And *Helium will carry a balloon for days. . . . But a hot-air balloon cools down in minutes.*

In addition, comparison is used to illustrate complex or technical terms by likening them to familiar or more commonplace objects. Thus, in the above example, since many people may not be able to visualize *30 cubic feet,* it is compared to something that is better known: *as big as a refrigerator.* And *30,000 cubic feet* is illuminated with the pictorial term *as big as three houses.*

"This comparison method is often used when I ask department heads to submit recommendations of prospective candidates to attend the prestigious Wright Conference on Strategic Problem-Solving Techniques," Fredricks said, handing Michael a memo with the work experience and strengths and weaknesses of candidates described in individual paragraphs.

TO: William Fredricks
FROM: Judy Hayes
DATE: October 31, 1991
SUBJECT: Two Candidates for the Wright Conference

After a thorough review of my supervisory staff, I would like to recommend two people from our department to attend the Wright Conference on Strategic Problem-Solving Techniques. They are Robert Mellow and Janet Armstrong. While I am pleased with the performance of both, I believe each is capable of substantial growth.

Bob Mellow joined the department 12 years ago. He does an excellent job when given clear, unambiguous instructions. But when a decision has to be made with incomplete information or under pressure — as, for example, during operational troubleshooting — Bob is uncomfortable and not at all at his best. Since he has no formal training as a supervisor or manager, I feel the conference will give him the decision-making skills he needs.

Janet Armstrong has about half the length of service that Bob has. She has been with the company a little over six years. But in that time she has frequently been the best person to have around when we are planning expenditures based on projected earnings. Her degree in mathematics provides a good basis for these analytical discussions. She makes decisions quickly and enjoys being in charge. But her aggressive style is sometimes difficult on her coworkers. Thus, she needs training to deal with the many personalities on her staff.

I am certain that Mellow and Armstrong will improve their managerial styles from attending the conference. And I am equally certain their experience will benefit our department. I am, therefore, pleased to recommend both as candidates to participate in the Wright Conference on Strategic Problem-Solving Techniques.

• The block comparison method is an excellent tool for writing recommendations or evaluations, since the people, places, or objects may be compared with one another in separate paragraphs. Take care, though, that the same characteristics are looked at in each example. Thus, if specific qualities of A are examined in one paragraph, then similar qualities of B should be described in another, of C in a third, and so on.

"A second comparison method, the point-by-point technique, helps writers keep a tight rein on their information," Fredricks said, showing Michael an article he had underlined.

THE U.S.: TEAM AT THE TOP OF NO. 2

A rumor has been circulating around Detroit for several months that Ford Chairman Donald Petersen, 61, will take early retirement so that Vice Chairman Harold "Red" Poling, who is 11 months older, can move up to chief executive officer before he retires too. Petersen swears he has no intention of retiring early, but the rumor points up the unusual degree of respect and cooperation between the two men.

Petersen and Poling are exemplars of Ford's new breed of manager. Both held big jobs overseas before landing top posts in the U.S. Petersen ran all of Ford's international automotive operations in the late 1970s, while Poling served as head of Ford's European activities for five years until 1980. They also are the prime movers behind the team spirit that has overtaken the company since the man with his name on the building, the late Henry Ford II, stepped down as chief executive in 1979.

Working together, Petersen and his red-haired colleague had a hand in Ford's first attempt at building a "world car." The effort foundered because the demands of European customers (small engines, high fuel economy) could not be melded with the wishes of American buyers (bigger engines, more optional equipment). But the project was the forerunner of the company's new policy of parceling out engineering assignments to separate "centers of excellence" on three continents.

In 1980 Petersen and Poling returned to the U.S., where Petersen was named company president and Poling got the job of reviving Ford's troubled North American operations. As the company's two top executives, they have done their jobs so well that Ford will make more money than GM and Chrysler combined this year, and Ford division cars and trucks have passed Chevrolet's as the biggest-selling individual brand.

At Ford's world headquarters, the two occupy adjacent offices and try to have lunch together once a week. Poling concentrates on operational matters, while Petersen focuses on strategic issues. In addition to desk time, both men spend at least four hours a month guiding cars around Ford's Dearborn test track to evaluate engines, transmissions, and suspensions. They were the first Ford executives to graduate from Bob Bondurant's four-day

performance driving course in California in 1982 — a cram
course in how to handle a car at high speeds and avoid accidents — and have been encouraging others to follow in
their skid marks. Poling, a finance man by training, says,
"It really helped me to learn about our products, to the
point where I can now make suggestions to improve them."

Around the company, the taller Petersen is known as
"Mr. Outside" for his unruffled behavior before large audiences, while Poling, who is considered fairly shy, does
better in smaller settings. Poling is the more competitive
of the two. Though he tore up a knee while playing college
football, he is an active golfer with a 7 handicap. Both
are collectors: Petersen of minerals and jazz recordings,
Poling of fine wine.

With Ford running as smoothly as an eight-cylinder
engine, a current concern for both men is picking their
successors. The odds-on candidate for chairman is Allan
Gilmour, 53, recently made head of international operations, while Philip Benton Jr., 58, who now runs the
worldwide auto business, and Louis Ross, 55, the North
American boss, are the leading candidates for the No. 2
job. Handicapper's tip: Look for two more men who can
work as a team.

The underlined words point out the similarities and
differences between the two men. Thus, Petersen ran all
of Ford's international automotive operations . . . while
Poling served as head of Ford's European activities. And
Poling concentrates on operational matters, while Petersen focuses on strategic issues. Around the company, the
taller Petersen is known as "Mr. Outside" for his unruffled behavior before large audiences, while Poling, who
is considered fairly shy, does better in smaller settings.
Poling is the more competitive of the two.

Phrases like working together and Both are collectors
are also ways of drawing comparisons.

- The point-by-point comparison method is valuable for writing performance appraisals and proposals. It is also an excellent technique for evaluating the pros and cons of a product. The performance of new products can be compared with older ones as well as with the brands of your major competitors. But each time you point out something about the new product, A, be certain to give the corresponding facts for product B, product C, and so forth. Compare each product cost for cost, strength for strength, risk for risk, etc.

The point-by-point comparison method is a useful technique for a memo on the results of a study on household gloves.

TO: W. Blaze, S. Conners, W. Fredricks, K. Robbins
FROM: Ted Coopers
DATE: November 10, 1991
SUBJECT: Household Gloves Study Report

I am sending you the report of the study that the consultant, ComPare, conducted on the three types of plastic household gloves we manufacture. ComPare tested for resistance to chemicals and punctures as well as for tactile sensitivity.

Chemical Resistance: Both the heavy- and medium-weight gloves were more resistant to motor and cooking oils and cleaning fluids than the lightweight gloves. The heavyweight gloves were also resistant to gasoline and turpentine, while the medium-weight gloves tended to become stiff and then crack after they were immersed in these substances.

Puncture Resistance: The heavyweight gloves performed best, as might be expected, in contrast to the thin, lightweight gloves, which offered almost no resistance when a device was used to measure the amount of pressure each sample glove could tolerate before a sharp object pushed through it.

Tactile Sensitivity: Both the heavy- and medium-weight gloves, which are textured or embossed, had better grips with heavy objects, such as iron cookware in soapy water. On the other hand, the lightweight gloves offered a good grip with small coins.

Recommendation: Based on the results of these tests, I recommend that production of medium-weight gloves, which stiffened and cracked, be discontinued. The heavyweight gloves were better for the tough jobs of serious clean-ups. The lightweight gloves had better tactile sensitivity for fine work, such as handling jewelry or silverware.

After you read the complete report, let's get together to discuss long-range strategy plans.

Argue with Cause and Effect

"The final structure on my menu is a popular one, too," Fredricks said. "The cause-and-effect pattern describes events or conditions and the conclusion that follows. Or it states a recommendation or result and then examines the facts that support that outcome."

TO: Users of Gambol Hall
FROM: Anne Peters
DATE: October 15, 1991
SUBJECT: Rescheduling of meetings

Starting November 1, Gambol Hall in Building B will no longer be available on Wednesday and Thursday afternoons. As a result, departments that usually hold meetings there on these afternoons will have to make other arrangements.

We regret any inconvenience caused by the change. Listed below are several options that might help in rescheduling your meetings:

North and South conference rooms in Building D
Room 612 in Austin
Meeting rooms in R&D

In this memo, the cause (unavailability of the room) and its effect (relocating of meetings) are simple, but the method is also a valuable technique for trying to persuade your readers of your point of view. Then the link between the cause and the effect must be established clearly with sufficient examples and factual evidence.

In Arthur Conan Doyle's short story "A Scandal in Bohemia," Sherlock Holmes says to Watson, "I see it, I deduce it. How do I know that you have been getting yourself very wet lately, and that you have a most clumsy and careless servant girl?" Holmes goes on to explain his conclusion by stating that it was simplicity itself: his eyes told him that on the inside of Watson's left shoe, just where the firelight struck it, the leather was scored by six almost parallel cuts. Obviously they had been caused by someone who had very carelessly scraped around the edges of the sole in order to remove crusted mud from it. Hence, the double deduction that Watson had been out in vile weather and that he had a particularly unsatisfactory boot-cleaning servant.

- Business memos frequently use deduction in a cause-and-effect memo aimed at persuading or convincing readers to take particular actions. How you present your facts and your examples can influence your readers' perception of your message.

TO: Executive Committee
FROM: Bill Fredricks
DATE: November 16, 1991
SUBJECT: Future Microwave Foods Development

I am recommending that our thrust in Research and Development this year be in the area of microwave foods.

Advances in food technology have expanded the kinds of convenience foods that can be prepared in microwave ovens these days. The packaging for certain frozen products has been designed to absorb high temperatures so that, for example, pizza crusts now brown nicely. Also, paperboard trays have been developed to eliminate an earlier problem of sogginess; the results are crispier fish and fried chicken.

Moreover, with supermarket freezer space getting tighter, we should also concentrate on microwave foods that do not require refrigeration. Soup mixes and pastas with sauces sealed from oxygen in plastic trays are good bets, since both items would be shelf-stable for 18 months. Consequently, they can be kept in a cupboard and taken anywhere — to an employee lounge or a school lunchroom.

Let me hear your thoughts before our next meeting.

- Cause-and-effect patterns are developed with words that lead your readers to anticipate that you'll be providing a reason or explaining a decision. Words such as *so that, because, moreover, since,* or *consequently* introduce a relationship and show how certain ideas connect to one another. Before drawing a conclusion or making a recommendation, the logic of your argument can be introduced with *the results indicate, it follows that, in conclusion,* or *to sum up.*

A good framework adds strength to your memos. The material in the memo on microwave foods development is presented in a cause-and-effect pattern. But using one structural design does not preclude the use of others as well. The topical arrangement of the paragraphs organizes the information by subject matter. The words *this year, these days,* and *now* provide a chronological sequence.

As Michael quickly reviewed the patterns for structuring information, he was struck by the common sense of the five patterns. He thanked Fredricks for sharing the secret of writing logical memos. "I guess my education's complete now," he said.

"Not by a long shot," Fredricks said, laughing. "You've learned ways of mapping your thoughts and choosing a structure. That's the second secret of good writing."

"What's the third one?" Michael asked.

"Good writing, you'll find, is largely a matter of rewriting. Even the best writers don't get it right the first time," he said, smiling warmly.

As Michael walked down the stairs, he wondered whether he would ever be able to write perfect memos.

(5)

Shaping Your Memo

- Throw out clutter
- Make your paragraphs lean
- Groom your sentences
- Build bridges that link ideas
- Brush up on grammar
- Put in periods and count your commas

You learn to write by writing, Michael thought. Forced to express his ideas on paper, he was gaining confidence. He was getting faster, too, so that twice a week he could spend his lunch hour in the company's workout center. One afternoon he saw Kate Vincent, jogging around the track. She was in charge of the company's benefits policy, and he often received memos from her. He was frequently impressed at how well she explained complicated ideas.

When they finished their laps, Michael told her that he admired the way she presented complex thoughts in a succinct form.

Kate thanked him. "Getting memos into shape is like

keeping physically fit," she said in her usual forthright manner.

"That's an interesting concept," Michael replied.

"Yes, it just takes exercising and good habits."

Throw Out Clutter

"What sort of exercises help you get your memos into shape?" Michael asked. Kate started back to her office and he walked beside her.

"After I write a memo, I throw out the clutter, those needless words that litter memos," Kate said. "Wordiness, like weeds in a garden, doesn't let your message grow. And it also stifles your readers' understanding."

"Can you give me an example of clutter?"

"Several." Kate stopped by the door of her office. "I've a collection culled from my own and other people's memos."

She took a manila folder from a filing cabinet and, flipping through it, took out a memo, which she handed to Michael.

TO: Distribution
FROM: C. S. Smith
DATE: November 12, 1991
SUBJECT: Employee Recommendations

I am taking the opportunity to write to you about my understanding of the real need to offer orientation in the work being done in other units of the company besides your own. Company tours are widely praised as providing an overview, but often there is a need to know more, specifically about the routines in another unit or units as they relate directly to your own job. Perhaps in the future we will be able to offer orientation to those who simply "desire" to know what is being done in another unit. In other words, we first have to address those having a "need" to know. By that I mean that your own job ties in with work being done in another unit of the company, and you see direct benefits for you in doing your own job if you receive orientation in that other unit.

If you feel this need, I would appreciate your completing and returning the attached form by November 18. I see this as a long-range program, but I would like us to begin in the month of December, if you indeed feel a need for such a program.

"Expressions such as 'I am taking the opportunity to write you about' or 'I would like to write you about' or 'It should be stated that' simply clutter a memo. Begin directly: 'I understand there is a need to offer orientation in the work done in units of the company besides your own.' That cuts a dozen extra words from the sentence," Kate explained.

"Writing 'in the month of December' instead of simply 'December' is puffery, too," she added.

"I'm afraid I suffer from that problem," Michael said, remembering his habit of using the expression "due to the fact that."

"Everyone does," Kate said with a smile. "If we stopped to analyze our expressions as we put them down, we'd become so self-conscious that we would write terribly stilted memos. Afterward, we need to examine our memos and edit ruthlessly. Writing is nine-tenths rewriting. Fine-tuning is the third step in writing good memos."

● Phrases such as *In other words* or *By that I mean* seldom clarify anything. Instead, they indicate that the writer was not able to express the idea clearly in the first place. And they lead readers to conclude that the writer must be an indecisive person.

Always check to see that every word does a useful job. Economy is very important in writing memos. People often fritter away their readers' attention with dull expressions. Never use a phrase when a single word will do. Be wary of the redundancy that creeps into memos: *absolutely complete, advance planning, end results, other options,* and *resume again.* And words that can be struck from windy expressions, such as the verbosity of *our check in the amount of* when *our check for* would do just as well. The inflated phrase *with the possible exception of* can be handled with the perfectly ordinary word *except.* The popular *at this point in time* crops up in memos, too. Writing *now* would be more to the point. After you write a memo, try this exercise: See how many unnecessary words you can cut from your draft without altering your meaning.

Make Your Paragraphs Lean

"It's like training with weights and improving your diet to get yourself into better shape. Exercise and good habits trim the flab from sentences, which in turn reduces the length of your paragraphs," Kate observed.

"How many sentences should be in a paragraph? What's a ballpark figure?

"There isn't an ideal length," Kate said. "About fifty years ago, writing had a more leisurely pace and paragraphs may have had twenty sentences or more. But in today's business world, I'm always thinking about how much my readers can absorb without needing a break."

Michael smiled. He was getting used to having people talk about keeping their readers in mind.

"The golden rule is to keep paragraphs short," Kate said. "A topic sentence and three or four others that give detail are generally sufficient. I find that nothing puts readers off as much as one solid wall of print after another. So even when there's a logical unity to the content, I divide paragraphs that become too long."

- First impressions are important. Creating white space on a page lets in the daylight. An occasional paragraph with a single sentence can make a strong impression.

Groom Your Sentences

"Most readers do better with sentences that are simple and direct, don't they?" Kate said. "But that isn't the way we think. When we've gotten up our momentum, we string along ideas, like clothes hung on a line, and connect them with ands, buts, and other conjunctions.

"Of course, you don't want all your sentences to have the same length and structure or else your writing will sound as boring as someone droning on in a monotone. The best way to capture your ideas is the way you hit a ball with a bat. Just swing without consciously thinking.

Afterward, though, you need to take a second look and groom straggly, unkempt sentences."

- Balancing several short sentences with a long one or vice versa gives your writing greater impact. Don't tag on conditions or qualifications that muddle your point. Put separate thoughts in separate sentences. The average length of a sentence should be between 15 and 20 words, based on counting all the words in a paragraph and dividing that figure by the number of sentences in the paragraph.

Government agencies are well known for clouding their writing with bureaucratic gobbledygook. The U.S. Department of Energy published the following Introduction in a brochure that was circulated to industry in 1978, when the agency was established.

THE PURPOSE OF DOE

The Department of Energy was established by Public Law 95-91 dated August 4, 1977, and was activated on October 1, 1977. The primary purpose of the Department of Energy is to achieve effective management of the energy functions of the Federal Government in meeting and solving the energy problem. This will be accomplished by providing a mechanism through which a coordinated national energy policy can be formulated and implemented to deal with the short-, mid- and long-term energy problems of the Nation; and by developing plans and programs for dealing with domestic energy production and import shortages. The Department of Energy will create and implement a comprehensive energy conservation strategy to carry out the planning, coordination, support, and management of a balanced and comprehensive energy research and development program and place major emphasis on the development and commercial use of solar, geothermal, recycling and other technologies utilizing renewable energy resources. The Department is also responsible for administering portions of the nuclear weapons program; improving the effectiveness and objectivity of a central energy data collection and analysis program; providing for cooperation with Federal, State and local governments; fostering and assuring competition and incorporation of material environmental protection goals in the formulation and implementation of energy programs.

The DOE is also charged with the responsibility of assuring that, to the maximum extent practicable, private enterprise is involved in the development and achievement of the policies and programs of the DOE. This is to be accomplished by fostering, insofar as possible, the continued health of the Nation's small business firms, municipal utilities, and private cooperatives involved in energy production, transportation, research, development, demonstration, marketing, and merchandising.

From the above you can see that we have a major challenge in meeting and overcoming energy problems. It is our firm belief that this can be accomplished by the joint efforts of the Federal Government and the industrial and academic communities.

The first paragraph, one and a half columns long, has an average of 40 words per sentence. Even for a person with a Ph.D., that sentence length is off the chart for readability.

An easy way to correct such sentences is to put the main facts in a short simple sentence and amplify your points in a second one.

The following revision divides the first long paragraph

into three paragraphs, with an average count of 20 words per sentence, and hones the total number of words in the paragraph to about half the original figure.

The Department of Energy (DOE) was established by Public Law 95-91 dated August 4, 1977, and was activated on October 1, 1977. Its primary purpose is to achieve a program that effectively meets and solves the nation's energy problems. This will be accomplished by providing a coordinated national policy to deal with short- and long-term energy problems. Programs will be developed to handle domestic energy production and import shortages.

To carry out the management of a comprehensive energy research and development program, the Department of Energy will create an energy conservation strategy. Major emphasis will be placed on the commercial use of solar, geothermal, recycling, and other technologies using renewable energy sources.

The DOE is also responsible for administering portions of the nuclear weapons program and improving the central energy data and analysis program. It provides for cooperation among Federal, State, and local governments; and fosters competition of material environmental protection goals in the formulation of energy programs.

The emphasis in your memos may often come from the variation you get in your sentences. Compare the government article on energy with the style of combining long and short sentences in the following paragraph from *Iacocca,* by Lee Iacocca with William Novak:

Fortunately, I wouldn't be starting from scratch. Chrysler had a long tradition of innovation, a tradition I was eager to continue. Not too many years earlier, a lot of young people had wanted a Chrysler because it was a hot item. Chrysler had Chargers and Dusters that ran down Main Street quicker than anybody's. Racing cars like high-winged Dodge Daytonas, the Chrysler 300 series, the Satellites and Barracudas were the ones that were clustered around drive-ins and hamburger stands from Maine to California.

Build Bridges That Link Ideas

Frequently writers know the logical relationship between one thought and those that follow, but they often fail to put in the transitions for their readers.

"If readers have to pause to understand the continuity of a memo, they may never find their way to its end," Kate explained. "Transitions are words, steppingstones, that help your readers see the connection between one thought and the next."

Michael rephrased the concept to clarify the idea for himself: "So we put in transition words because they help our readers see the link between the points in our memo."

"You've just done it! Before giving the reason, you said 'because,' " Kate exclaimed.

• Transitions foreshadow what will be coming next. Some writers put in these connecting words spontaneously as they organize their ideas. Giving an example, they may preface it by *in particular, namely,* or *for instance.* Developing an idea, they may write *furthermore, hence,* or *thus.* Drawing a comparison, they may point to it with words such as

similarly, both, or *in contrast.* And stating an oppo-
site point of view, they may warn their readers with
but or *on the other hand.* These connecting words add
coherence to your writing by tying together the ideas
in your sentences and paragraphs.

Taking an article from her folder, Kate said, "Professional writers use transitions all the time. I underlined
the connecting words in this paragraph from an article
called 'Household Worries.' "

With ominous regularity, evidence keeps popping up that
one chemical after another — <u>often</u> unrecognizable to the
ordinary citizen — poses a threat to human health. <u>Usu-
ally,</u> the toxic compounds directly affect only particular
groups of people, <u>such as</u> chemical workers or farmers.
<u>But</u> last week, two authoritative agencies pointed accus-
ing fingers at <u>two</u> chemicals that are part of everyday life.
The Department of Agriculture threatened to prohibit the
use of sodium nitrite as a preservative in bacon, ham,
sausage and other meats, <u>since</u> it could be a cancer-
causing threat. <u>And</u> the nonprofit Environmental Defense
Fund called for strict regulation of 2,4-diaminoanisole sul-
fate, a component of permanent hair dyes that may be
linked with cancer.

Usually, often, and *such as* indicate that an example
will be forthcoming, while *two* shows a comparison. *But*
at the start of the third sentence warns readers of a
change from "particular groups of people" to "part of
everyday life." And *since* leads readers to expect that a
reason will be given. *And* at the beginning of the final
sentence signals that a point will be added.
"Here's a memo in which I underlined the transitions

that help the flow of the writing. They let readers glide
easily from one thought to the next," Kate said.

TO: Distribution
FROM: Ted Packard
DATE: September 17, 1991
SUBJECT: Travel Policy

The Company relies on your fairness in planning business
trips with the same care you would use in arranging your
personal travel.

In most cases, we ask that you take coach accommodations. If you choose to use your own car for business travel,
you will be reimbursed at the rate of airline or other public
transportation coach fare. On the other hand, if you use
your automobile because you need to carry passengers or
equipment that is difficult to transport by public means,
you will be paid at the set rate per mile for the actual
distance traveled.

Costs for meals, hotels, and other expenses should be kept
within the limits suggested by the "Guide for Travel,"
published by our office. Since reimbursement for food and
lodging will be on an actual cost rather than a per diem
basis, we ask that travel vouchers be submitted with original receipts for any expenditures over $25.

Transition words take advantage of your readers' expectations. A brief reference forward or back is generally
enough. But if they are omitted, the memo sounds choppy
and less friendly. *In most cases* connects the second paragraph to the first one and prepares readers for an example. *On the other hand* indicates an opposing point will
be stated. *Because* leads readers to anticipate a reason.
Since also signals that an explanation will follow.

Of course, transitions won't help if the logical relations are missing from the thought process. The connection must first be there. But whether your readers fully understand your points depends on your guiding them from one thought to the next. Good business and professional writers use transitions all the time to build bridges that link their ideas for their readers.

Brush Up on Grammar

Although memos are less formal than letters or reports, basic grammatical principles should still be followed.

"We plan our paragraphs," Kate said, "but often our sentences simply evolve. We string our thoughts from subject to verb to object and include whatever else comes to mind. For example: 'John, the personnel manager, hired Robert, who was bright and capable with figures, after he interviewed other candidates, because he claimed he was the best person for the job.' "

"Yes, I see. The sentence grew," Michael said.

"One thought suggested another. I always check the reference of pronouns to their antecedents."

Michael frowned. "I've forgotten about antecedents."

"In the final clause, *because he claimed he was the best person for the job,* it isn't clear whether the initial 'he' refers to the personnel manager or the candidate for the job. It would be better to write: 'John, the personnel manager, hired Robert, who was bright and capable with figures, after he interviewed other candidates. The personnel manager claimed John was the best person for the job.' "

- Pronouns are substitutes for people, places, or things that were named earlier. Review your memos to be certain that the relationship of the pronoun to the earlier reference is not ambiguous. In particular, watch out when you start a sentence with a pronoun such as *this, that, these,* or *those;* all too often the previously mentioned reference may be vague or obscure.

"Review your memos for subject-verb agreement, too," Kate said. "Of course, everyone knows a singular subject takes a singular verb and plural subjects take plural verbs. Problems come up when it's not obvious whether the subject is singular or plural. Then you need to know the rules.

"Keeping the subject and verb close to each other makes it less likely that a singular subject will be used with a plural verb and vice versa."

"What about data?" Michael asked.

"I know some people insist it should be used only with a plural verb. They claim that's the way it's been for two thousand years. But data as a singular collective noun is now considered acceptable," Kate said. "The way I see it, language is dynamic, always changing."

- Grammar is the gymnastics of good writing. Use proper English. Careless mistakes can make your readers think that you don't know any better, that you don't care, thereby undermining your credibility.

Put In Periods and Count Your Commas

The old virtues of correct spelling and proper punctuation are the nuts and bolts of clear memos. Punctuation marks aren't just a convention. They're like traffic signals and help the flow of your memo.

Periods indicate the end of a complete thought and thus give readers a chance to pause and absorb what has been said. Unfortunately, many writers don't put in enough periods. Their sentences are too long for busy readers. Learn to use periods to make your points.

Commas baffle lots of people. Sprinkle them lightly, because they have a habit of growing in memos. Commas, like flashing signals, should be used with discretion. If the traffic is slight, you can safely leave them out. In heavier traffic, commas help avoid bottlenecks by setting off:

· Independent clauses — complete thoughts — joined by a conjunction, such as *and, or, but, not, for.*
· Clauses or phrases at the start of a sentence.
· Items in a series.
· Words or phrases that may be omitted without any loss of meaning.

Semicolons come between two independent clauses to show that the ideas are closely related. Some people link two independent thoughts with a comma; that's called a run-on sentence or a comma splice.

Colons tell your readers to proceed ahead. They introduce an explanation, a list, or the main body of a letter after the salutation.

"I would be happy to send you exercises on grammar and punctuation," Kate said.

"I'm sure that would help get my memos into shape," Michael said, thanking Kate again for her assistance.

A few days later he received a packet from Kate. In it were exercises for cutting the flab from his writing, lists of connecting words and phrases for making logical shifts from one idea to another, thoughtful exercises on basics, and refreshers on commas and other tips on punctuation marks.

Michael performed the exercises carefully. Then he put them in a notebook as handy reference sheets.

(6)

Listening to Your Memo

- Hear your own voice
- Be yourself
- Use the active voice
- Show your feelings
- Practice modulating your tone

One morning Michael arrived at his office to find the following memo in his in-box:

TO: All Users (and Abusers) of Parking Privileges
FROM: Your Conscience
DATE: December 15, 1991
SUBJECT: Annual Speech

Amid a cacophony of angry muttering it is about time for the annual speech! There are over 200 people working in this building and 10 visitors' parking slots. Visitors' parking slots are just that — spaces for visitors to our office and delivery people. They are not the private purview of a privileged few (those being the people with a lot of chutzpah or the luck to get there first).

It is convenient for those of us who work here to park in the visitors' area occasionally for a few hours. No one has the right to park there all day every day. Now no one likes the idea of calling in security to ticket or tow. But it is not out of the question — it has been done! We should be able to handle this matter intelligently ourselves. You're bright enough to remember your car belongs in the regular parking area most of the time. End of speech!

Michael read the anonymous memo several times. He wondered who had sent it. It certainly didn't sound like his boss, so he walked over to Carter Craig's office. "What am I to make of this?" he asked.

"What *do* you make of it?" Carter responded.

"It's not particularly effective. The writer refers to 'time for the annual speech,' so it's not the first memo that's gone out on the subject. Besides, I'm annoyed by the accusation since I don't park in the visitors' spaces. I call it country club management. 'We should be able to handle this matter intelligently by ourselves,' " Michael quoted. "With the ultimatum about calling security. 'It has been done!' And that comment about being 'bright enough.' There's a pretense of good humor, but underneath a raging current of anger. It's very sarcastic!"

"You're getting good at hearing between the lines of a memo," Carter said.

Hear Your Own Voice

Attitudes can be heard in the written word, just as in face-to-face discussions. Skilled business writers don't risk offending their readers. Even if they have a gripe, they keep anger and sarcasm out of their memos.

"How would you have dealt with the issue?" Michael asked.

"Matter-of-factly. And I would have added a line of politeness, something I might say in conversation," Carter said, scribbling on the memo:

TO: Everyone
FROM: Carter Craig
DATE: December 17, 1991
SUBJECT: Visitors' Parking Spaces

The visitors' parking area is meant primarily for visitors to our office and delivery people. At times, everyone finds it convenient or necessary to park in a visitors' space for a few hours. But there are over 200 people in the building and only 10 visitors' slots. So use the regular parking area most of the time. Thanks for your cooperation.

"Listening to your voice lets you hear the way you sound to others. Read your *own* and other people's memos out loud," Carter suggested. "Often what readers think is pleasant or dull, sarcastic or self-important, read with interest or remember easily, is largely a matter of modulating your tone."

"Tone?" Michael echoed.

"The way your readers 'hear' you," Carter said. "Whether you sound serious, clever, interesting, reasonable, trustworthy, ponderous, expert, witty, and so forth."

• Train your ear to be sensitive to your readers. Unfortunately, there are no handy formulas for testing the reaction your words produce (unlike the way you measure the complexity of your prose by counting the number of words and sentences in a paragraph or recognizing that short, simple words are easier to understand than longer ones). After you've written a memo, read it aloud. You may be surprised by what you hear.

Be Yourself

"Good memos have personal warmth," Carter said. "When I began writing memos, they were stiff and a bit pompous. Then I noticed that some memos seemed a good deal more downright human than mine. They weren't pretentious and artificial. I admired those memos and wondered how their writers achieved their effect."

"And how did they?" Michael asked.

"They chose words and expressions that sound friendly," Carter said. "Someone once wrote to me, 'I hate burdening you with more report reading, but I would appreciate your looking this over and giving me your assessment.' Another time I got a memo that read, 'Please glance at this report and give me a phone call or scribble me a note in the near future. Many thanks and apologies for the imposition.'

"I remember them because I was impressed by their informal and congenial tone. I recognized that 'I would appreciate your looking this over and giving me your assessment' wasn't the same as 'Many thanks and apologies for the imposition.' What occurred to me afterward was that these writers were being themselves."

● We all have different vocabularies. Words are like
foods. They can be spicy, flat, sharp, sweet, tart, foreign, and even unfamiliar. Just the way you have
leverage in organizing your thoughts, you have freedom in your choice of words.

Carter took a rather tattered, thin book off the shelf
behind him. It was a book on traditional business writing
he'd found in a secondhand bookstore, *Martine's Sensible
Letter-Writing*, which had been published in 1866, just
after the Civil War. Michael read several samples.

Application for the Position of Conductor
Gentlemen:
    I feel very desirous of obtaining a situation as conductor
on the railroad under your control. I believe myself fully
competent to fulfill all the duties of the place, having been
for several years engaged in a similar position in the employ of the New Jersey Central Railroad Company. Your
attention to the accompanying testimonials from the president and chief engineer of the company just named is
respectfully solicited, and assuring you that if I obtain
the situation I seek, I will endeavor to show my sense of
the obligation by a zealous and diligent discharge of my
duties.
    I remain, gentlemen,
      Your obedient humble servant,

Testimonial
Gentlemen:
    Finding that Mr. Alexander is a candidate for a situ-
ation in your house, I beg to say that during the two years
he was in my employ I had every reason to approve highly
of his character and services. Mr. A's principal duty was

that of first salesman in my establishment, and while he kept my interests steadily in view, his polite manners and obliging disposition secured the good opinion of my customers. Mr. Alexander has frequently assisted me in the selection and purchase of goods, in which department his knowledge and taste were of great value. He is qualified to conduct correspondence, and is expert and accurate at calculations. Should any further particulars regarding Mr. A. be required, it will afford me pleasure to communicate the same on application.

> I am, gentlemen,
>> Your most obedient servant,

"They've got an arcane style. They're well written, but they're genteel," Carter said. "It may appear strange, but your creative right side 'hears' an overrefinement in those letters that sounds artificial to our ears today. Of course, the direct and informal tone that we now use might seem blunt and ill-bred to writers from the nineteenth century. We're all prisoners of our time and culture, but allowing for that, our writing creates an impression that is more than the sum of our words."

Carter looked directly at Michael. *"Be yourself. Be yourself. Be yourself,"* he admonished sharply.

Some writers use worn-out expressions and trite phrases that have completely lost their meaning. They write "as per your order," "attached please find," "awaiting the favor of your reply," "pursuant to our conversation," "thanking you in advance." They couch their memos in stock business phrases that don't reflect their personality and that sound as outmoded as letters written a century ago.

- Here's a tip for developing self-awareness in your memos. Try asking yourself, "How would my friends be likely to respond to this if I said it aloud?" If you suspect they would ridicule your choice of certain phrases or laugh at a hyperlegal expression, practice expressing yourself in a simpler and more forthright manner.

Use the Active Voice

"Some memos sound as though a computer instead of a real person cranked out the message. I can probably convey what I'm talking about if I show you an example," Carter said, fishing a memo from his in-box.

Michael read quickly with interest.

TO: Carter Craig
FROM: T. G. Dooley
DATE: December 12, 1991
SUBJECT: New Account Numbers

As part of our continuing effort to provide the best and most convenient service, our processing system is being upgraded so that it can handle transactions faster and more efficiently than ever before. In order to accommodate our system enhancement, in certain instances, new account numbers have been issued to some departments.

Enclosed is a temporary supply of our order forms which have been encoded with a new account number. In order to eliminate confusion, please destroy any current forms and begin using our new forms immediately.

"The memo's written in the passive voice. Many people worry that their writing sounds undignified or unprofessional or immodest, so they put their sentences in the passive voice."

"The passive voice?" Michael frowned.

" 'Our processing system is being upgraded' rather than 'we are upgrading our processing system.' Or 'new account numbers have been issued' instead of 'we have issued new account numbers,' " Carter explained. "No one takes responsibility for the action. The passive voice puts distance between the writer and the act."

• The passive voice is an evasion strategy that produces dry, impersonal, and ineffectual writing. For example, "It was noticed that an error occurred on your recent statement. An adjustment will be made immediately." Who made the adjustment? No one! The thoughtful writer would have said: "We are sorry for the inconvenience this error caused you and we will make an adjustment immediately." Be an involved writer! Use the active voice.

Show Your Feelings

"Sometimes people get so immersed in what's happening in their own department, they write their memos completely from their own point of view," Carter observed. "Take another look at the memo from the accounting department. It doesn't aim for any common ground. It's written totally from the standpoint of Dooley's interests: 'our continuing effort,' 'our processing system.' The personal pronoun 'you' is completely missing from the memo."

Michael counted five 'our's and not a single 'you' in the memo.

"As for the business jargon, it's not much different from the old-fashioned kind. 'System enhancement,' indeed! I don't know what that is! Plus those unfriendly phrases: 'in order to eliminate,' 'in order to accommodate,' " Craig said.

- Memos shouldn't have the flat, neutral tone that's used in making a reservation at a hotel or ordering a piece of equipment. Memos are generally going to people you know well, or at least moderately well, and so should strike the same friendly note that's part of your other relationships.

"Let me show you the memo I got from the publications office," Carter said. "Compare it with the one from the accounting department."

TO: Carter Craig
FROM: Tim McCallisher
DATE: November 28, 1991
SUBJECT: Design Schedule

A belated thank-you for inviting me to discuss your department's publication needs. I have studied the materials you gave me, together with your timetable.

I propose working on a new logo that would be appropriate for most of your products. Once it is approved, the logo would become an integral part of all your publications. I expect to show you some designs and applications by mid-January. If you are happy with them, I would proceed to do your brochure for your March mailing date.

I hope this schedule meets with your approval, and I'll give you a call in a few days to discuss details.

"As you can see, McCallisher includes me in the message," Carter said, indicating the sentences: "I have studied the materials *you* gave me, together with *your* timetable." "I expect to show *you* some designs. . . ." "If *you* are happy with them. . . ."

"Even though memos are written hastily and not expected to be as polished as a letter or report, you want to get the same feeling in them that comes through when you're dealing with someone directly," he said, pointing out that the memo from the publications office started in a friendly manner: "A belated thank-you for inviting me to discuss your department's publication needs."

- The secret of writing a friendly memo is letting your readers know you're interested in them. When you talk to someone in person or on the telephone, you begin or finish with a greeting or some pleasantry, don't you? Why not do the same thing in a memo? Of course, memos don't have salutations or signature lines, but a personal word or two at the beginning or end serve the same purpose that they do in conversation.

"I never know whether I should include a person's title or not," Michael said. "Should I be writing 'Mr. William Fredricks, Senior Vice President, Packaged Foods'?"

"Normally we're less formal in memos than in letters, so titles are omitted. But it's a good idea to identify people by their full names to avoid having a message go astray.

Of course, you might tag on a person's title as a sign of your respect," Carter said, "just as you might use a tone that's deferential when you talk directly with a senior person in the company."

"What about initialing memos?" Michael asked. "Some people do and others don't."

"Memos don't have a complimentary close, so they don't require a signature. But many writers initial their memos to indicate that they have seen and approved the message."

• A markedly courteous tone in a memo reflects the attitude you would have if you were talking directly to senior members in the company. Don't write *In my opinion* or *Let me call your attention to*. Instead, *I am recommending* or *May I suggest* is heard as more appropriate. On the other hand, when the responsibility is yours, it is as important to convey your attitude that the decision is yours. Choose a tone that is polite but firm.

Quite often you're under a good deal of time pressure when you're preparing a memo, so you don't have the leisure to make prolonged revisions. Keeping your reason for sending a memo in mind often helps you find the right tone.

Sharing concerns. When you talk, you recognize similar objectives. You may say "I understand your attitude about" or "I share your interest in." That same respect for common goals should come through in your memos.

Taking responsibility. When you talk, you admit a mistake occurred. You are likely to say "I'm sorry about that error" or "I apologize for the oversight." Even when you were not personally responsible, you respond with sympathy and helpful suggestions. That same thoughtfulness and understanding should be reflected in your memos.

Showing appreciation. When you talk, you tell people when they have done something that pleases you. You are inclined to say "Thanks for your help with" or "I value your suggestion on." That same expression of gratitude should be part of your memos.

Saying "no" nicely. When you talk, you turn down a request gently. You might say "We regret that our present tight budget doesn't allow . . ." or, contradicting someone's opinion, "No one would have predicted it, but based on previous results. . . ." That same tactfulness should appear in your memos. But never be dishonest. Don't write "It's company policy and there's no way around it" and then get caught red-faced doing the same thing for someone else.

Memos often fall into specific categories. The type of memo that you're writing can sometimes point to an appropriate tone.

- *Adjustment or apology memos* are written because something has gone wrong and needs to be corrected. Accept responsibility. Explain that you are sorry about the error and are taking steps to see that a similar mistake does not happen again. Your tone should be sincere, straightforward, and understanding.
- *Complaint memos* are sent when the error or problem occurred someplace else. Tell clearly and briefly what has happened and what needs to be done to correct the

situation. Aim for a tone that is polite and matter-of-fact, never angry or sarcastic.

- *Congratulatory memos* acknowledge an achievement or milestone. Not everyone writes such memos, but sending them to people who have received a special award or been given a promotion is a friendly act. To someone retiring from the company, mentioning past accomplishments and future plans adds a positive and personal note.
- *Courtesy memos* express gratitude to people who have been especially helpful or extended themselves for you. Send a thank-you memo promptly and refer to specific actions or reasons for writing the memo. Be warm and natural; write "Thanks for your help" or "I enjoyed working with you" or "Let's get together soon."
- *Follow-up memos* provide facts, figures, and other pertinent information. Consider what your readers want and need to know, then come to your point quickly. "I looked into the questions you raised," or something similar is a good start. You should sound direct and businesslike.
- *Recommendation memos* give your opinions. Rate the characteristics of the person, product, or situation evenhandedly. Do not ignore flaws or problems, but at the same time never be condescending or hostile. Appraisals should be fair. Omitting all criticism may make a recommendation seem less than candid. And remember that an unperceptive recommendation reflects on the writer, too. Keep your tone forthright and honest.

Practice Modulating Your Tone

Often the words people choose are different from the impression they want to make. Readers may hear something in a memo its writer didn't intend — a choice of words or phrases used repeatedly that reinforce an image.

"The most practical advice I can give you about writing memos is to collect memos that sound good to you. Read them aloud. Listen to how you sound in your own memos, too," Carter said. "And practice modulating your tone."

> • *Be positive.* Words such as *reject, decline, contradict, deny, refute,* and *dispute* sound cold and disagreeable and rankle in your readers' ears.
>
> *Be good-humored.* A witty remark can be just the thing to cool an overheated situation, but don't be flippant or sarcastic. You may end up offending your readers.
>
> *Be honest.* Your style and tone will emerge naturally from what you have to say. That doesn't mean that the memo won't have faults. But as you keep trying to express yourself sincerely, the barriers to expressing what's on your mind will come down.
>
> *Never exaggerate!* Even the most factual statements have hidden agendas, so write your memo with restraint. A single magnified comment, tossed off lightly, may cause your readers to suspect everything you wrote previously.

Here are two exercises that will help you practice listening to your voice:

Write three versions of a memo requesting a member

of your staff to come to see you in your office. Don't reveal the reason for the meeting, but keep it in mind as you write your memo. Your hidden agenda is to
(a) suggest working on a project,
(b) inform about a promotion,
(c) reproach for poor performance.
Afterward, read your memos aloud and see if you can hear the differences in your tone.

Write a complaint memo and then turn the tables by replying to it yourself. As you read the memos aloud, how do you see yourself? Put attitudes you find agreeable in one column and those that strike you as unpleasant in a second. Here are a few you might look for:

friendly?	hostile?
serious?	pompous?
understanding?	unreasonable?
cordial?	condescending?
witty?	sarcastic?
sincere?	evasive?
forceful?	argumentative?
straightforward?	pretentious?
tactful?	boorish?
supportive?	uptight?
respectful?	opinionated?
agreeable?	superior?
natural?	stiff?
lively?	dull?
polite?	arrogant?

• At one time, memos were brief interdepartmental communications exchanged strictly within the com-

pany, form packaging slips accompanying goods that
were shipped, or sometimes unsigned, diplomatic
communications. But technology has changed all
that. Electronics drives the office now, and the interdepartmental memo isn't just an internal communication anymore.

"About a decade ago, there were predictions that information technology was going to turn us into a paper-
less society. Instead, computer-based technology has led
to more and more people expecting hard-copy printouts,"
Carter commented philosophically. "In a short ten years,
information that would have been discussed on the phone
is now put into a computer, printed up, multiplied on
copiers in a matter of seconds, and sent off via E-mail or
faxed to someone in your own building, in a branch office,
or in another company halfway around the world.

"This new technology reinforces the demand for traditional writing skills. The clock may have supplanted
the sundial and the compass the need to chart by the
stars, but these computer-based instant data systems are
simply communication tools, not one iota different from
the typewriter or the telephone."

"Well, does sending memos outside the company affect
getting the friendly tone we've been talking about into
our writing?" Michael asked.

"Getting a memo with warmth and personal style is
pleasing everywhere," Carter replied with a smile, "and
is always valued in business messages."

(7)

Writing a Memo

About a month after their discussion about getting the right tone in a memo, Carter Craig stopped by Michael's office.

"I've had complaints lately from people who have trouble reaching our department because the lines are often busy," he said. "It seems to me two or three people spend an inordinate amount of time on the phone in what appears to be social conversation. A brief reminder of company telephone policy might be in order."

Brainstorming on the Computer

Michael had gotten used to putting down his uncensored thoughts and no longer tried to get a perfect first sentence. Instead, he imagined he was talking to the screen. He knew that writing a first draft was like scribbling ideas on a pad. First drafts weren't for anyone else to see. So he jotted down the points he wanted to cover, writing his ideas in fragments of sentences without thinking about their order or whether there were typos and mistakes in grammar. If he found he was going too far astray, he broke off in the middle of a sentence and started over again. He knew he could adjust the nuts and bolts of spelling and punctuation later on. Get it out and then get it right, he remembered hearing Kate Vincent say. Writing in this way, he got down several paragraphs in ten minutes.

Then he leaned back in his chair and read the words. He saw at once that some sentences could be simplified and certain words omitted. Also, many of his ideas did not have proper transitions and were not flowing logically. He quickly deleted repetitions that were part of his natural thought process, substituting words that made his sentences stronger and more concise. Then he made a road map with numbers and drew arrows to give the memo a clearer order.

It has recently come to my attention that....not
attention....boring word....Recently I have become aware of
customers having altogether too much difficulty reaching this
department due to busy telephone lines. Even though company
policy is entirely explicit with regard to telephone use, up
until now we have been quite lenient in enforcing this policy.
In spite of that it would seem that two or three people are
gabbing too long in what are obviously windy, private
conversations. I would like to reiterate company policy
concerning use of the telephone. Let me remind you that the need
to make urgent calls arises only occasionally. Even local calls
tie up the lines....discussions with credit card agencies, repair
men people....planning vacations.... An occasional call is
allowed permitted--otherwise personal calls are against the
rules. The complaints which have recently reached my desk make
it necessary for me to repeat company policy and to ask everyone
to be more aware of their telephone habits.

~~It is everyone's responsibility to obey the rules~~. Please
review company policy in relation to phone usage. ⓐ Personal
telephone calls are not ~~allowed.~~ .permitted during working hours
unless something unexpected comes up. 2. Necessary local calls
should be kept brief and long-distance calls should not be
charged to the company. Remember that a customer who isn't able
to reach our department will call our competition.

Revising a Memo

Then Michael revised the draft on his computer. The new
version looked like the earlier draft, but he had settled
on the major points, grouped similar ideas in paragraphs,
and set up a writing route.

Recently I have become aware of a number of complaints
from callers who are experiencing difficulty reaching this
department, because the telephone lines are frequently
busy. Even though company policy is clear about telephone use, all people in the department are asked to become more aware of their telephone habits.

Let me remind you that urgent personal calls will come
up occasionally, but it seems several people are gabbing
on the phone in what are obviously windy, private conversations. I would like to reiterate company policy concerning use of the telephone. Even local calls such as
discussions with credit card agencies, repair people, or
travel agents tie up the lines. An occasional call is permitted — otherwise personal calls are against the rules.

Please review company policy in your personnel manual:
1. Personal telephone calls are not permitted during
working hours unless something unexpected comes up.

2. Necessary local calls should be kept brief. 3. Long-distance calls should not be charged to the company. I realize everyone needs to make personal calls, but keep in mind, too, that a customer who isn't able to reach our department will call our competition!

Michael set his memo aside to let his thoughts rest and incubate. He knew that when he looked at the memo again, even a short time later, he would find that he had a fresh perspective.

Above his desk he had posted a checklist:

Turn on the ignition
Cruise with my passengers
Consult the road map
Choose the quickest route
Check the nuts and bolts
Adjust personal tone

As he looked over the different points, he realized he hadn't set up any common ground between his passengers and himself. He read his memo aloud, thinking, I might tie in more with my readers' experience . . . cut the sarcasm about gabbing on the phone, too.

Carter Craig had told him to include his reader in his message, so Michael imagined writing to someone in the department whom he could count on to react. "How do I want to come across?" he asked himself. Fair and understanding, he hoped. And firm, too.

With these thoughts in mind, he wrote the memo a third time.

TO: Department Staff
FROM: Mike Perkins
DATE: January 20, 1992
SUBJECT: Telephone Use

Recently I was told that callers have difficulty getting through to our department because our lines are frequently busy. I'm sure you agree it's important to have our phones lines available for business calls.

It's useful to remember to:

· Make only required personal calls during working hours.
· Keep your personal calls brief.
· Clear personal long-distance calls with your supervisor before making them.

I understand you need to make special calls sometimes — everyone does — but reducing the length and number of personal calls to a minimum helps. Thanks for your assistance.

Before Michael sent off the memo, he showed it to Carter. He had gotten strong enough to take his boss's suggestions and criticism in a way he could not when he began.

Carter smiled and said, "Persuasive writing, more than any other form, requires taking a middle ground. Your memo works because you've written it in a reasonable way. Too often writers overstate their case."

"I thought if I wanted to get my readers' cooperation, I should put myself in their place. First I wrote about urgent phone calls coming up occasionally, but not gabbing in a long-winded, private conversation. Then I added, 'I realize everyone needs to make personal calls.' But when I tried seeking their help, I looked at it from their point of view and wrote, 'I understand you need to make special calls sometimes, everyone does.' Actually, I revised my memo three times."

"That's the only way. Write and then rewrite. Writing skills, like many others, take practice."

"The pain's beginning to ease," Michael admitted.

Carter nodded. "There's lots of benefits to being able to write well. Brainstorming your thoughts. Organizing your ideas. Getting your personality into a memo. You've mastered the process now. You're going to be an important part of our team."

A few days later, Michael went to see Kate to show her his notebook and its summary of the steps to persuasive business writing. He had not been to her office for several months. He noticed that the cartoon on the wall behind her desk was still there and that the spider plant in her window had several babies. His own plant wasn't doing too well. When he was stuck in his writing, he overwatered it; then, when he was busy organizing his thoughts, he neglected it. But that wouldn't happen anymore.

(8)

In Summary

Getting Started

- **WARM UP WITH AN EXERCISE**
  Write quickly for ten minutes without stopping to edit.
  Don't try to be logical. If you miss a point, backtrack
  and explain yourself.

- **TALK TO YOUR READERS**
  Pretend you're having a conversation. Jot down your
  thoughts in phrases or sentence fragments. Use words
  that are part of your everyday vocabulary.

- **CAPTURE ALL YOUR THOUGHTS**
  Don't censor yourself. If digressions come to mind,
  write them down. They may contain valuable ideas.

- **BE IMPERFECT**
  Turn off the critic. Don't worry about clumsy phrases
  and awkward expressions. They're part of your original
  thought process.

- **PLAY WITH YOUR IDEAS**
  Get it down; then get it right. Remember, it's easier to
  write and revise than stare at a blank sheet of paper
  or an empty screen!

Focusing on Your Readers

- **LET YOUR THOUGHTS INCUBATE**
  Set aside your first drafts for a short time. Hook into the right hemisphere of your brain — your intuitive thinking — to get a fresh perspective.

- **BECOME YOUR READERS**
  Write the first draft of a memo for yourself; then turn it around for your readers. Remember that writing is a two-way process. Anticipate and respond to questions your readers will ask.

- **TELL WHY YOU'RE WRITING**
  Target your information. Make the opening sentence in a memo read like the headline of a newspaper.

- **RECOGNIZE YOUR KEY IDEAS**
  Pick out your major points. They're the scaffolding of your memo.

- **BE SPECIFIC**
  Pin down your abstractions. Describe your key ideas in ways your readers can picture.

- **DEFINE YOUR CODE WORDS**
  Share your code words with your readers. Use your technical terms, business jargon, acronyms, and abstract expressions as jumping-off points to explain your key ideas.

Planning Your Memo

- **PREVIEW YOUR POINTS**
  Brief your readers at the outset on *everything* you'll cover in your memo. Remember, busy people often get interrupted while they're reading a memo.

- **GROUP SIMILAR IDEAS**
  Cluster your ideas into categories that become the focal points of your paragraphs.

- **SET UP A WRITING ROUTE**
  Post road markers to lead your readers in the right direction. Use headings, topic sentences, and visual cues to lead your readers to important stopping places along the way.

- **MAP YOUR MIND**
  Draw a free-form diagram to help you organize your thoughts. Order your ideas.

- **DEVELOP SHARED GOALS**
  Present your ideas in an order that solves problems or achieves ends your readers care about. Know your readers' mind-set.

Choosing a Structure

A structure underlies all good writing. Select one of these structures, or a combination, to help your readers follow the pattern of your thoughts.

- **ARRANGE BY TOPIC**
  Tell the main points of the paragraph in the first sentence; then develop and refine the subject. Provide factual information, typical instances, and supporting data. Useful for developing an idea by themes.

- **HIGHLIGHT WITH PARALLEL CONSTRUCTION**
  Express similar ideas in a similar form. This symmetry makes it easier for your readers to understand your points. Handy for giving brief instructions or setting up agendas.

- **RELATE IN CHRONOLOGICAL SEQUENCE**
  Present information in a sequential order through words related to time, such as *at present, initially, later,* or *first, second, third.* Tell the background of a problem or the status of a situation. Practical for describing a process, a meeting's progress, a lab report, the history of an organization, or an ongoing matter.

- **DRAW COMPARISONS**
  Examine and highlight similarities and differences. Useful for writing proposals, making recommendations, or evaluating people, products, or situations.

- **ARGUE WITH CAUSE AND EFFECT**
  Begin with specific examples and end with a general conclusion. Analyze factors that led to decisions, recommendations, or results. Helpful for drawing logical

conclusions or making precise recommendations based on a number of examples.

Shaping Your Memo

- **THROW OUT CLUTTER**
  Watch out for redundancies and other windy expressions. Avoid overwhelming your message with wordiness.
- **MAKE YOUR PARAGRAPHS LEAN**
  Divide long paragraphs even when there is a logical unity to the content. Create white space on the page to let in the daylight.
- **GROOM YOUR SENTENCES**
  Aim for short sentences. Don't tag on conditions or qualifications that cloud your point.
- **BUILD BRIDGES THAT LINK IDEAS**
  Use transitional words and phrases to make logical connections. Help your readers understand your points by placing steppingstones that go from one point to the next.
- **BRUSH UP ON GRAMMAR**
  Keep within the bounds of accepted English. Be cautious with basics: the relationship of the subject to its verb, the pronoun to its antecedent, and the principles of proper word usage.
- **PUT IN PERIODS AND COUNT YOUR COMMAS**
  Pay attention to punctuation — it is more than a convention.

Listening to Your Memo

- **HEAR YOUR OWN VOICE**
  Listen to the way you come across to others: watch out for anger and sarcasm. You should avoid both tones in your memos. Train your ear to hear between the lines of a memo.

- **BE YOURSELF**
  Don't be pretentious or artificial. Choose fresh words that mirror your attitudes. The English language offers a wide variety; words, like foods, can be spicy, flat, sharp, sweet, tart, foreign, and even unfamiliar.

- **USE THE ACTIVE VOICE**
  Be an involved writer. Form sentences with subjects that take action and are responsible. Don't write in a dry, bureaucratic fashion that sounds as though a computer cranked out the message.

- **SHOW YOUR FEELINGS**
  Project a friendly picture of yourself. Let your readers know you care about them. Use the personal pronoun "you" often. Keep your purpose for writing the memo in mind to help you find the right tone.

- **PRACTICE MODULATING YOUR TONE**
  Watch for words and phrases used repeatedly that reinforce an image you may not have intended. Listen to how you sound: put tones you find agreeable in one column and those that strike you as unpleasant in another. Try responding to your own memos.

Appendix

Index

Appendix

Simplify, Simplify

Always check to see that every word is useful. Never use a phrase when a single word will do.

VERBOSE	IN A WORD
Absolutely complete	Complete
Advance planning	Planning
Afford an opportunity	Let
Am in receipt of	Have
A number of	Some
As a means of	To
At all times	Always
At an early date	Soon
At such time as	When
At the present time	Now
At this point in time	Now
Because of the fact that	Because
By means of	By
Continue to remain	Remain

VERBOSE	IN A WORD
Despite the fact that	Although
Due to the fact that	Because
During the time that	While
End result	Result
For a period of	For
For the purpose of	For
For the reason that	For
Has the ability to	Can
In an effort to	To
Inasmuch as	Because
In close proximity	Near
In order to	To
In receipt of	Have
In regard to	About
In the amount of	For
In the event of	If
In the near future	Soon
In view of the fact	Because
Make inquiry regarding	Inquire
Of the opinion	Believe
Perform an analysis of	Analyze
Pertaining to	About
Place an order for	Order
Prior to	Before
Provided that	If
Relating to	About
Subsequent to	After
Until such time as	Until
With reference to	About
With the exception of	Except

EXERCISE: CONCISENESS

Avoid redundancies and windy expressions. Substitute a word for a phrase whenever possible.

1. We are unable to fill your order due to the fact that there has been a dock strike.
2. I am writing in response to some questions that have arisen with respect to the recent announcement that there will be an increase in the charge for the use of the copiers.
3. I am enclosing herein my report for the month of December.
4. In regard to the new rating system that will be going into effect, there are two points that must be clarified in order to ensure that we can be as selective as possible.
5. The following statistics serve to support my personal opinion with reference to pension planning.
6. The data conclusively shows that Cereal 206 is a more superior product.
7. Every administrator seems inclined to agree with the concept that time is money.
8. It was the first time in my life that I attended a conference on sharing costs.
9. We are in receipt of your check in the amount of $4,500.
10. A few of the participants left the room early before the chairperson adjourned the meeting.
11. In Chicago, he had at least six different jobs.

ANSWERS

1. We are unable to fill your order because of the dock strike.
2. I am responding to questions about the increase in the charge for the use of the copiers.
3. I am enclosing my December report.
4. Two points about the new rating system must be clarified to ensure that we can be as selective as possible.
5. The following statistics support my opinion about pension planning.
6. The data conclusively shows that Cereal 206 is a superior product.
7. Every administrator agrees that time is money.
8. It was the first time I attended a conference on sharing costs.
9. We are in receipt of your check for $4,500.
10. A few participants left the room before the chairperson adjourned the meeting.
11. In Chicago, he had at least six jobs.

Avoid Business Jargon

Use simple, everyday words instead of the polysyllables that have become common currency in business writing.

BUSINESS CLICHÉS	PLAIN TALK
Accommodate	Hold, provide
Accomplish	Complete
Accurate	Correct
Acknowledge	Recognize
Adjacent to	Next
Administer	Manage
Admonish	Warn
Allocate	Set aside
Ambiguous	Unclear
Ameliorate	Improve
Anticipate	Expect
Appoint	Name
Appreciate	Value
Approximately	About
Ascertain	Find out
Attempt	Try
Benefit	Help
Cognizant	Aware
Collaborate	Work together
Commence	Begin
Competent	Capable
Comply with	Follow
Component	Part
Comprise	Make up
Conception	Idea

BUSINESS CLICHÉS	PLAIN TALK
Concerning	About
Consequently	As a result
Constitute	Form
Contain	Have
Convene	Meet
Cooperate	Work together
Coordinate	Rank, arrange
Currently	Now
Deem	Believe
Demonstrate	Show
Depart	Go
Designate	Name
Discrepancy	Difference
Disseminate	Distribute
Divulge	Tell
Duties	Work
Elect	Choose
Eliminate	Remove
Employ	Use
Encounter	Meet
Endeavor	Attempt
Endorse	Support
Ensue	Follow
Equitable	Fair
Equivalent	Equal
Establish	Prove
Esteem	Respect
Execute	Carry out
Exhibit	Show
Exigency	Need
Expedite	Hasten
Expunge	Erase

BUSINESS CLICHÉS	PLAIN TALK
Exterior	Outer
Fabricate	Make
Facilitate	Aid
Feasible	Possible
Fortunate	Had the good luck
Fulfill	Carry out
Generate	Produce
Immediately	At once
Impact	Effect
Inaugurate	Start
Indicate	Show
Initiate	Begin
Innovation	Change
Inquire	Ask
Inquiry	Question
Institute	Start
Intention	Aim
Maintain	Keep up
Manifest	Obvious
Manufacture	Make
Methodology	System
Modify	Change
Notify	Inform
Objective	Goal, aim
Observe	Notice, see
Obtain	Get
Operate	Run
Option	Choice
Parameter	Limit
Participate	Join, take part
Perform	Do, carry through
Permit	Let

BUSINESS CLICHÉS	PLAIN TALK
Prearrange	Arrange
Presently	Now, at this time
Previously	Before
Procedure	Way
Proceed	Go on, continue
Procure	Buy
Proficient	Skilled
Provide	Supply
Purchase	Buy
Recapitulate	Sum up
Reflect	Think
Regarding	About
Remuneration	Payment
Render	Submit
Request	Ask
Require	Need
Rescind	Take back
Reside	Live
Selection	Choice
Shortcoming	Flaw
Solicit	Seek, ask for
Submit	Send
Subsequent	Later, following
Sufficient	Enough
Suitable	Fit
Transmit	Send
Transpire	Happen, occur
Ultimate	Final
Usage	Use
Utilize	Use
Validate	Confirm
Viable	Possible

Be Sensitive to Your Readers

Remember, memos are sent to men and women who have diverse backgrounds and experiences. Avoid writing "he" and "his" unless you are referring to a specific person. Instead, rephrase the sentence to use the plural pronouns *they* and *their*. For example, instead of "Everyone should submit his expense account by Friday noon," consider "Staff members should submit their expense accounts by Friday noon." In cases where a singular pronoun is required, *he or she* is preferable to *he/she:* "He or she will be responsible for analyzing our recordkeeping needs."

In addition, avoid gender-specific titles and terms.

INSTEAD OF	TRY
Businessman	Business executive or manager
Cameraman	Camera operator
Chairman	Chairperson or chair
Congressman	Representative or senator
Foreman	Supervisor
Girl/guy Friday	Office assistant
Mailman	Mail carrier
Manpower development	Human resource development
Pressman	Press operator
Salesman	Salesperson
Spokesman	Spokesperson
Stewardess	Flight attendant
Stock boy	Stock clerk
Tradesman	Shopkeeper
Workman's compensation	Worker's compensation

Physical characteristics, age, and ethnic background should not be mentioned unless they are relevant to the job description or your message. Focus on the individuals and their accomplishments. If you do refer to disabilities, gender, or particular groups, be sensitive and informed.

INSTEAD OF	WRITE
Older manager	Manager
Petite secretary	Secretary
Short salesman	Salesperson
55-year-old programmer	Programmer
Female engineer	Engineer
The deaf	People with hearing impairment
The handicapped	People with disabilities
Cripple	Person with a disability
Diabetic	Person with diabetes
Wheelchair-bound	Wheelchair-user
Oriental	Person from China or Japan, etc
Indian	Native American

Words That Sound Alike

The spelling checker on your computer cannot tell whether you have chosen the proper meaning for some common business words.

ACCEPT/EXCEPT

The controller cannot *accept* unauthorized vouchers.
(*Accept* is a verb meaning "to receive willingly.")
All travel vouchers will be paid *except* bar bills.
(*Except* as a preposition means "with the exception of.")

AFFECT/EFFECT

The cold weather *affected* sales adversely that month.
(*Affect* is a verb meaning "to influence.")
Only the board of directors can *effect* a change in the company's pension plan.
(*Effect* as a verb means "to bring about, make happen.")
The *effect* of the vote was no increase in taxes.
(*Effect* as a noun means "result.")

ALL READY/ALREADY

Finally the papers were *all ready* to file with the commissioner.
(*All ready* used adjectivally means "completely prepared.")
The papers were *already* in the mail when the commissioner telephoned.
(*Already* is an adverb meaning "previously, by this time.")

ALL TOGETHER/ALTOGETHER

The computers were set up *all together* in the large area on the second floor.

(*All together* means "collectively in one place.")

The sales conference was long but *altogether* worthwhile.

(*Altogether* is an adverb meaning "entirely, completely.")

ASSURE/ENSURE/INSURE

The personnel director *assured* the young man that he would be promoted at the end of the year.

(*Assure* is a verb that means "to make secure or certain by setting a person's mind at rest.")

Safety goggles are regulation gear to *ensure* that the staff will be protected against unforeseen accidents.

(*Ensure* is a verb meaning "to make secure or certain from harm.")

The company cars were *insured* against theft or fire.

(*Insure* is a verb meaning "to make secure or certain, or to guarantee life or property against risk.")

COMPLEMENT/COMPLIMENT

The colored photographs will *complement* the text and provide a better understanding of the technique.

(*Complement* as a noun or verb means "adding to complete or bringing to perfection.")

After the conference, the director *complimented* the staff for a job well-done.

(*Compliment* as a noun or verb means "expressing praise.")

COUNCIL/COUNSEL

The town *council* met to vote on the issue.
(*Council* is a noun meaning "a group of people, elected or appointed, who meet to consult or deliberate.")
The president and vice-president of the company hired a lawyer to *counsel* them on the best way to proceed.
(*Counsel* as a noun or verb means "providing advice or guidance.")

ITS/IT'S

The company has *its* main headquarters in Cincinnati.
(*Its* is the possessive form of the pronoun "it.")
Now *it's* time to say a few words about vacation schedules.
(*It's* is the contraction of "it is" or "it has" and is used in informal writing or in dialogue.)

PRECEDE/PROCEED

Mr. Johnson talked longer than any of the speakers who *preceded* him.
(*Precede* is a verb that means "to come before in time or occur prior to.")
Their lawyer advised them on the best way to *proceed*.
(*Proceed* is a verb that means "to move on or go forward, especially after stopping.")

PRINCIPAL/PRINCIPLE

Mr. Clark played the *principal* role in the negotiations.
Ms. Stout prefers to live frugally on the interest from her investments rather than touch her *principal*.
(*Principal* as an adjective means "first or foremost in importance." As a noun it refers to the person in charge

or leader, especially of a school; in the financial sense, as capital or a sum of money owed as a debt.)

Mr. Howe bases his decisions on the old-fashioned *principle* that virtue is its own reward.

(*Principle* is a noun pertaining to basic truths or fundamental laws.)

STATIONARY/STATIONERY

Interest rates depend on many factors and are seldom *stationary*.

(*Stationary* is an adjective that means "fixed in position, not moving.")

Their office *stationery* is very distinctive: pale gray paper with lavender envelopes.

(*Stationery* is a noun meaning "writing paper.")

Bridges That Link Ideas

Use connecting words and phrases to build bridges that
make logical shifts from one thought to another.

CLUES THAT TAKE THE READER FORWARD

Adding an example:	and, especially, for example, for instance, for one thing, in general, in particular, namely, occasionally, often, specifically, such as, that is, to illustrate, usually
Providing a time sequence:	afterward, as soon as, at last, at the same time, before, by, finally, first, initially, in the meantime, later, meanwhile, next, now, once, originally, presently, recently, second, since then, subsequently, then, until
Establishing place:	at the front, farther back, in the distance, in the foreground, in the rear, to the center, to the east, (north, south, west), to the left (right), up front

CLUES THAT DEVELOP AN IDEA

Adding a point:	also, and, and then, furthermore, in addition, in fact, moreover, not only/but also, or, second, third
Adding emphasis:	above all, all in all, and so, chiefly, equally important, even more so, indeed, more important, obviously
Conceding a point:	after all, although, and yet, at the same time, certainly, despite the fact, doubtless, even though, granted, no doubt, of course, still, though, to be sure, whereas, yet
Giving a reason:	because, for, hence, it follows, since, so, then, therefore, thus
Returning to a point:	even so, nevertheless, notwithstanding, still
Reversing a thought:	but, however, in spite of, not at all, on the contrary, surely, yet

CLUES THAT DRAW COMPARISONS

Showing similarities:	and, also, better, between, both, each, likewise, more, similarly, together, two

Pointing out differences: conversely, despite, different, even though, in contrast, instead, on the other hand, still, than, while

CLUES THAT SUM UP POSITIONS

Introducing a conclusion: accordingly, as a result, consequently, finally, in conclusion, on the whole, so, therefore, thus, to sum up

Punctuation: Stop and Go

Periods (.) mark the end of a declarative statement or an abbreviation.

Question marks (?) are placed at the end of an interrogative sentence.

Exclamation points (!) punctuate emphatic statements.

Semicolons (;) are stop signs between two independent clauses or between a series of terms that already contain commas.

Colons (:) are green lights that signal the reader to proceed. They introduce an explanation, a series or listing, or the main body of a letter after the salutation.

> Three words can be used to define Directive Behavior: STRUCTURE, CONTROL, and SUPERVISE. Different words are used to describe Supportive Behavior: PRAISE, LISTEN, and FACILITATE. (*Leadership and the One Minute Manager,* by Kenneth Blanchard, Patricia Zigarmi, Drea Zigarmi)

Commas (,) signal the reader to pause or watch for road construction. The following six rules cover their elementary usage:

1. Place a comma after each term in a series of three or more.

> He turned on the light, opened his log book, and began to record his expenses.

Omit the comma if one word in the series modifies another one.

> She wore a new, plain, dark brown blouse.

2. Place a comma after introductory clauses or participial phrases.

> When Ann reviewed the figures, she found an error.
> Reviewing the travel deductions, our auditor found many unwarranted expenditures.

3. Use a pair of commas to set off nonrestrictive or parenthetical expressions.

> Ms. Smith, our lawyer, filed the brief.
> Mr. Hanger, who is a CPA, audited the figures.
> Priority issues, arising in our discussion, were settled.
> Mr. Jones, I am certain, will attend the meeting.

Omit the commas when the clauses or phrases identify which person, place, or thing is meant.

> The man who analyzed the figures is our accountant.
> Issues arising in our discussion were settled.

4. Use a comma to set off words that require a pause or introduce a sentence.

> First, let me apologize for the error.

5. Place a comma before a conjunction that introduces an independent clause unless the clauses are brief.

The early records of the company are stored in another building, and it would take several hours to find them. You read and I'll check the figures.

6. Use a comma when more than one prepositional phrase comes at the start of a sentence.

During her first day at the plant, Alice met several co-workers.

Dashes (—) are detours to inserted or added thoughts.

Another reason is that governments, with rare exception — Brazil is the most important one — resist the truth about inflation. (*Managing in Turbulent Times,* by Peter F. Drucker)

Parentheses [()] enclose digressions. (The punctuation is inside the parentheses if a complete sentence is enclosed.) Otherwise, when a phrase or clause is put in parentheses (whether relevant or not), the punctuation is placed outside the parentheses.

Ellipses (. . .) indicate that a thought or quotation is incomplete.

Quotation marks (" ") set off direct conversation, titles, and quotes by other writers.

Hyphens (-) connect the parts of compound words and are used when a word could otherwise be misread.

Free-lance writer, part-time employee, pre-empt

Subject-Verb Agreement

Names of organizations and business firms always take a *singular* verb.

Cromwell and Shields has its offices in New York City.
Sitwell Systems publishes a reference manual on toxic waste materials.

Compound subjects take a plural verb.

The book and the magazine are on my desk.

Correlative conjunctions (either/or; neither/nor; not only/but also) take:
A. A *singular* verb when *both parts of the subject are singular*.

Neither Ms. Forest nor her secretary knows the policy on job sharing.

B. A *plural* verb when *both parts of the subject are plural*.

Either pastel *tones* or fiesta *colors come* in that series.

C. A verb *that agrees with the closer subject* when one part of the subject is singular and the other part is plural.

Not only several coach *seats* but also a first-class *ticket is* available on that date.
Neither the marketing *department* nor the sales *offices have* openings in January.

Collective nouns (army, audience, class, club, committee, crowd, group, jury, orchestra, public, quarter, team) generally are considered *a unit* and take a *singular verb.* When *individual members* are thought of as acting separately, then a *plural verb* may be used.

> The marketing *team is* launching an advertising campaign in October.
> The marketing *team are* disagreeing among themselves about launching the advertising campaign.

Indefinite or compound pronouns may be either singular or plural.
Singular indefinite or compound pronouns (anybody, anyone, anything, each, every, everybody, everyone, everything, nobody, no one, nothing, somebody, something) take a *singular* verb.

> *Everyone* in the finance offices *knows* the deadline for filing tax returns.

Plural indefinite pronouns (both, few, many, others, several) take a *plural* verb.

> *Several* in the accounting office *know* the regulations for filing a late return.

Intervening phrases or clauses that come between subject and verb are *sidestepped* so that the verb agrees in number with the subject of the sentence and not with the nouns in the phrases or clauses. (Keeping subject and verb close to one another makes it less likely that a singular subject will be used with a plural verb or vice versa.)

The *catalogue* on gardening tools *is* now obsolete.
The *reports* that Jim wrote about our new product *are* complete.

Inverted subjects require careful reading. Normally the subject of a sentence comes before the verb. When that order is reversed, be sure to find the subject of the sentence and make certain the verb agrees with it.

Displayed on the bulletin board of the cafeteria *are photos* taken at the company's annual picnic.

Put in its simpler order, the sentence would read:

Photos taken at the company's annual picnic *are* displayed on the bulletin board of the cafeteria.

Mathematical expressions (percentages, portions, and fractional) take *verbs that agree with the noun in the phrase.*

Sixty percent of the *members were* present.
Some of the *orders were* shipped.
Two-thirds of the *report was* finished.

EXERCISE: SUBJECT-VERB AGREEMENT

1. The players on the team (is/are) from the accounting department.
2. The file on James and Smith (takes/take) two drawers.
3. The report and the statement of the people involved (has/have) been submitted.
4. One-quarter of the offices (is/are) occupied.
5. Several of the group (eats/eat) in the cafeteria every day.
6. Included in his baggage (was/were) a tape recorder, a microterminal, and our latest price list.
7. To all the volunteers who helped make the day a success (goes/go) our heartfelt appreciation.
8. Everyone in the department (agrees/agree) on the strategies for the promotional campaign.
9. (Is/Are) the filing cabinet and the copier machine in the same area?
10. Neither Mr. Johnson nor his sales staff (sees/see) any reasons to make changes.
11. The committee (votes/vote) on all changes affecting personnel policy.
12. An analysis of the extent to which computers (is/are) used by the sales group (leads/lead) me to conclude that less time (is/are) spent in the drudgery of filling out forms.

ANSWERS

1. are	4. are	7. goes	10. sees
2. takes	5. eat	8. agrees	11. votes
3. have	6. were	9. are	12. are, leads, is

Index